P9-BYL-069

Better Homes and Gardens®

step-by-step
yard care

Better Homes and Gardens® Books
Des Moines, Iowa

Better Homes and Gardens® Books
An imprint of Meredith® Books

Step-by-Step Yard Care
Writer: Liz Ball
Project Editor: David Haupert
Art Director: Lyne Neymeyer
Copy Chief: Catherine Hamrick
Copy and Production Editor: Terri Fredrickson
Contributing Copy Editor: Chardel Blaine
Contributing Proofreaders: Sue Fetters, Nancy Ruhling, JoEllyn Witke
Principal Photographers: Derek Fell, Saba S. Tien
Contributing Photographer: Dency Kane (page 11)
Indexer: Janel Leatherman
Electronic Production Coordinator: Paula Forest
Editorial and Design Assistants: Kaye Chabot, Mary Lee Gavin,
  Karen Schirm
Production Director: Douglas M. Johnston
Book Production Managers: Pam Kvitne, Marjorie J. Schenkelberg

Meredith® Books
Editor in Chief: James D. Blume
Design Director: Matt Strelecki
Managing Editor: Gregory H. Kayko
Executive Garden Editor: Cathy Wilkinson Barash

Director, Sales & Marketing, Retail: Michael A. Peterson
Director, Sales & Marketing, Special Markets: Rita McMullen
Director, Sales & Marketing, Home & Garden Center Channel: Ray Wolf
Director, Operations: George A. Susral

Vice President, General Manager: Jamie L. Martin

Better Homes and Gardens® Magazine
Editor in Chief: Jean LemMon
Executive Garden Editor: Mark Kane

Meredith Publishing Group
President, Publishing Group: Christopher M. Little
Vice President, Consumer Marketing & Development: Hal Oringer

Meredith Corporation
Chairman and Chief Executive Officer: William T. Kerr

Chairman of the Executive Committee: E. T. Meredith III

All of us at Better Homes and Gardens® Books are dedicated to providing you with information and ideas to enhance your home and garden. We welcome your comments and suggestions. Write to us at: Better Homes and Gardens® Books, Garden Editorial Department, 1716 Locust St., Des Moines, IA 50309-3023.

If you would like to purchase any of our books, check wherever quality books are sold. Visit our website at bhgbooks.com.

Copyright © 2000 by Meredith Corporation,
Des Moines, Iowa.
All rights reserved.
Printed in the United States of America.
First Edition.
Printing Number and Year: 5 4 3 2 1   04 03 02 01 00
Library of Congress Catalog Card Number: 99-75941
ISBN: 0-696-21030-4

Cover Photograph: C. Colston Burrell

contents

If you're a first-time

homeowner, or even a renter with a

yard you have to care for, *Step-by-Step*

Yard Care is the book for you. And it's so easy to use! ❧We've

organized the book by plant groups—starting with lawns—so

you can turn easily to that chapter and see what you need to do.

introduction

We also offer chapters on lawn

alternatives (including groundcovers and vines), trees and

shrubs, and creating a great front yard. At the end of each

chapter there's a checklist of related chores for both northern and

southern gardeners. And the yard basics section shows and

describes the tools to use for different tasks, how to fertilize, and

more. ❧You'll find everything you need to know to keep your

yard looking great—from patching a lawn to choosing trees for

four-season interest. With more than 30 step-by-step projects and

100 timesaving tips to guide you, you'll have a great looking yard

before you know it.

Happy Gardening!

Cathy Wilkinson Barash
Executive Garden Editor

lawns

selecting grasses

For the best-looking, easiest to maintain lawn, plant varieties of grasses that are well-suited to your climate and the intended use of the lawn. Recent research by seed companies and universities has led to the introduction of many improved varieties of lawn grasses. Some are more resistant to insects and diseases than older varieties, while others are more tolerant of shade, drought, or heavy wear. Check with your local Cooperative Extension Service or local nurseries to find out about varieties adapted to your area. Lawn grasses are classified as either cool season or warm season. ¶Cool-season grasses are generally adapted to northern climates, where they grow vigorously in

Kentucky bluegrass is best suited to full sun in areas with cold winters. In fact, it is one of the most cold-hardy grasses, often used in public parks. It needs regular watering to make it through dry periods. Kentucky bluegrass is prized for its thick dense turf and fine texture. Some of the best of the new varieties include 'America', 'Blacksburg', 'Blue Star', 'Chateau', 'Eclipse', 'Julia', and 'Midnight'.

spring and fall and may turn brown in very hot summers. They are often sold as a blend of several varieties of the same species, such as several varieties of Kentucky bluegrass, or as a mixture of two or more different species such as Kentucky bluegrass and fine fescue. Growing blends or mixtures is a good idea—if one or more of the varieties doesn't grow well or is destroyed by disease, chances are that the others will take over and flourish. The most common cool-season grasses include fine fescue, Kentucky bluegrass, perennial ryegrass, and tall fescue. The new varieties

reading the labels

When you shop for grass seed, be aware of some of the descriptive terms used. Low maintenance means that it will grow with a minimum of . watering and feeding. Disease resistant implies a grass that will grow and thrive even where disease-causing fungi abound. Many will be resistant to certain diseases, but not all. Greenup refers to the time (usually spring) when the grass breaks its dormant spell (this could even be from heat in summer), starts to grow quickly, turns lush green—and needs mowing.

9

selecting grasses (cont'd.)

of Kentucky bluegrass, unlike the old standards, are quite disease-resistant, and keep their fine-textured looks without a lot of feeding and have some drought tolerance. Fine fescue includes several grasses—chewings fescue, hard fescue, and creeping red fescue—that are often mixed with Kentucky bluegrass as they thrive in shade and drought. Perennial ryegrass is one of the main components of cool-season grass mixes. It germinates quickly and wears well. Warm-season grasses are adapted to the South, growing best in hot weather, and going brown and dormant when temperatures dip to freezing. Zoysiagrass is the most winter hardy of the southern grasses and is sometimes grown to Zone 7. It stays brown all winter in cooler climes, however, and is slow to greenup in spring.

If you like the relaxed look of a longer lawn, grow tall fescue. The new varieties make a wonderful low-maintenance lawn—they are drought-tolerant and stay green all season in sun or shade without feeding. Don't mix tall fescue with other grasses. A warm-season grass that will perform equally well is buffalograss, which grows to just 4 inches without mowing. Although it doesn't require feeding or watering, it can turn brown in extremely hot or cold weather.

It's a dense grass that's somewhat tolerant of shade and grows best in the upper South. Bermudagrass is suited to Florida and the Gulf Coast and thrives when it gets abundant water. It wears well, staying green longer than other warm-season grasses. St. Augustinegrass is a coarse grass, adapted to the humid coastal areas of the South. It is not tolerant of freezing weather or much shade but stands up to sun and high traffic. Bermudagrass is common to the mild-winter West Coast and southern regions. Some varieties can be started from seed, while others are grown only from sod or sprigs.

Water the lawn in the daytime so the blades of grass can dry out in the warmth of the sun, thus preventing infection with fungus. In cold climates, a mix of fine fescues with Kentucky bluegrass is best in areas with dappled shade. In southern regions, Bahiagrass is the lawn of choice, growing even in poor, sandy soil. However, it is susceptible to dollar spot, brown patch, and mole crickets.

laying a sod lawn

Turfgrass sod is an attractive option when it's time to renovate a tired old lawn or put in a new one. It's an instant fix and, when properly installed, eliminates problems with soil erosion, mud, and weeds. And you can lay it almost any time during the growing season. ❧Professionally raised grass in high-quality sod is sturdy and dense from the outset and is usually weed-free. You can find sod in several of the most common grasses for your area. Although the initial cost of sod is considerably more than grass seed—especially if you hire a contractor to lay it—seeding costs about the same in the long run since you have to overseed in spring and fall following the initial seeding to grow a dense lawn.

YOU WILL NEED

- shovel
- organic matter
- granular fertilizer
- rake
- fresh sod
- water
- wheelbarrow/cart
- kneeling board
- sturdy knife

weather

For best results, lay sod in the spring or fall when there's likely to be more rainfall to help the lawn become established. However, you can patch bare spots in existing lawns any time of the year that the ground isn't frozen. Be prepared to water often during the hot summer months.

1 Establish a bed an inch below grade so the new lawn will be even with walkways. Dig organic material and slow-acting, granular fertilizer into the soil, then rake the bed smooth and level.

2 Store the sod in the shade; keep it rolled and moist until you're ready to use it. Bring one or two rolls at a time to the site in a wheelbarrow or cart. Moisten the soil bed just before laying the sod.

4 Lay subsequent rows so the end seams are never flush with those of adjacent rows. Coax the edges as close together as possible, but don't stretch them.

5 Don't stand on newly planted sod; instead use a kneeling board to lay additional rows. Use a sturdy knife to cut sod to fit irregular spaces.

Laying a sod lawn is an expenditure of time and money. ❧ Think of your lawn as a garden of grass. Before planting, prepare the soil as you would any garden bed. Add plenty of organic matter so the soil will retain moisture, yet drain well. Aerate it to encourage microbial activity. Once the sod is planted, deep watering is essential—the water must penetrate 6 inches below the sod—to encourage roots to penetrate deeply as they knit the sod to the soil. Pay attention to the seams between pieces of sod and the edges along walks and drives and water them carefully because they dry out quickly.

3 Lay the first length of sod along a straight edge such as a sidewalk. Unroll the grass strip gently, placing it snugly against the walk. Start the second roll of sod so its end neatly abuts the first.

6 Tamp the sod, or gently use a roller to establish good root contact with the soil. Fill any gaps with loose soil. Generously water the entire lawn.

choosing sod

Fresh, healthy sod is the key to a successful sod lawn. Because the grass in commercial sod is professionally grown in top-quality soil that receives regular fertilizing and watering, it is sturdy, dense, and weed-free. Sod should be newly harvested—ideally within a day before it's laid. Arrange for it to be delivered as soon as you've finished preparing the soil. The sod will arrive piled on pallets in rolled or folded strips, with the soil side exposed. The strips of sod are generally 1 to 2 feet wide and 4 to 10 feet long. Unroll a strip to inspect it. The grass should be at least 2 inches long and of a uniform green color. The soil on the underside should be dark and moist, about 1 inch thick, and show a tight matrix of healthy roots. Store the pallets in the shade. Keep the pieces of sod moist, and cover them to avoid drying out in case there's an unexpected delay.

Sod is available in many types of grass. If you're doing a patching job, try to find a sod with grass that resembles the color and texture of the grass surrounding the patch. When in doubt, compromise by choosing a mixture of grass types. An advantage to sodding is that it gives you an opportunity to introduce a new grass blend or mixture that's appropriate for your site. If it's an area that gets a lot of foot traffic, use a mixture that features tall fescue, which stands up best to wear and tear. Or if the area is primarily for display, a blend of Kentucky bluegrasses may look elegant.

starting a lawn from seed

Sowing grass seed is the most common method of starting a new lawn of cool-weather grasses. Grass seed is relatively inexpensive and covers a large area of prepared soil quickly. Buy the best quality seed so you can benefit from all the latest technology in breeding sturdy, disease-resistant grasses. ❦ Seed mixtures combine several kinds of grasses such as Kentucky bluegrass, tall fescue, and perennial ryegrass in various proportions. Their respective weaknesses offset each other to assure a green lawn all season. Blends, on the other hand, combine several varieties of the same kind of grass, such as three types of Kentucky bluegrass, to provide a uniform look. Local nurseries and garden centers

YOU WILL NEED

- shovel
- organic matter
- rake
- granular, slow-acting fertilizer
- seed
- water
- polyspun garden fabric or straw

1 Careful preparation of the soil is critical to the success of a lawn grown from seed. Clear out all vegetation, then dig in some organic material to improve the soil's ability to hold moisture.

2 The grass seed must touch the soil, so remove any stones and debris that you find. Using a garden rake, smooth out the soil; be sure to eliminate any dips or bumps.

5 After about a week of weeding, it's time to sow the grass seed, following package instructions. Water lightly to moisten the seed and soil.

6 Mulch the newly seeded area to protect the seed. Polyspun garden fabric or straw helps maintain essential moisture in the seed bed.

carry formulations appropriate for your region. ◥The keys to success in growing a lawn from seed are proper timing, good preparation, and aftercare. Fall is the best time to sow cool-weather grass seed. In zones 5 to 7, for example, sow seed around Labor Day to give the grass time to extend its roots deeply into the soil so it can endure the heat of summer. ◥The healthier the soil, the better the lawn. Prepare the soil two weeks before you sow the seed to allow time to get rid of emerging weeds. Water faithfully and plan to add more seed the following year so your new lawn will be dense and plush.

liming lawns

In certain regions, the soil is more acid than grass prefers. If you live in such an area, spread dolomitic or granular limestone on the lawn. It takes effect in about 3 to 6 months. Lime is alkaline, so it neutralizes excess acidity, sweetening the soil. Never fertilize and lime a lawn at the same time. The combination produces ammonia gas, releasing the fertilizer's valuable nitrogen into the air.

15

3 Spread granular, slow-acting lawn fertilizer evenly over the soil. Be sure to follow package instructions for application. The fertilizer provides uniform, consistent nutrition over several months.

4 Rake the fertilizer into the soil to rough it up and make a good seed bed. Add water and wait for several days for any newly surfaced weed seeds to sprout and grow. Remove the weeds.

7 For optimum germination, keep new grass seed constantly moist. Seedlings will penetrate straw or push up the light garden fabric as they grow.

8 Keep watering, less frequently but more heavily, as roots continue to grow. When the seedlings are 3 inches tall, remove the fabric and lightly mow.

using plugs and sprigs

Warm-season grasses, such as Bermudagrass, zoysia, or St. Augustinegrass, are usually planted as sprigs or plugs because they don't set viable seed. Starting a lawn with these individual plants is much less expensive than using regular sod, although both sprigs and plugs are rooted pieces of sod. ▼Sprigs are thin 3- to 6-inch pieces of grass stems or runners without soil.

Plugs are 2- to-4-inch chunks of sod, either round or square, with soil around their roots. ▼Spring is the best time to plant sprigs and plugs. Before planting, prepare the soil well. Till or dig in organic matter and add granular, slow-acting fertilizer. Smooth out the soil with a rake. ▼The biggest

planting plugs

YOU WILL NEED

- plugs
- shovel
- organic matter
- fertilizer
- rake
- trowel
- water

1 Buy fresh plugs and keep them moist. Clear the site of weeds, stones, and debris. Dig in some organic matter and granular, slow-acting fertilizer, then use a rake to make the soil smooth and level.

2 Plant plugs as soon after purchase as possible. Set them on the soil equidistant from each other in a grid pattern. The closer together they are, the sooner the grass will spread to form turf.

3 Dig a hole for each plug, deep and wide enough to accommodate its root system. Set plug in hole and gently press soil over roots and against crown.

4 Water the plugs well and often. Eliminate weeds that sprout between them. Mow when the grass is 3 inches tall to stimulate it to spread.

problem you'll face will be weeds. Digging the soil brings weed seeds to the surface—they'll sprout wherever there is bare soil the minute they're exposed to sun and moisture. Because there's a lot of bare soil between the sprigs or plugs of grass for quite a while, it's worth the time and effort to deal with the weeds first. Water the prepared soil and allow a week or two for the weeds to sprout. Remove or kill the weeds, then plant the grass, disturbing the soil as little as possible. During the time it takes the grass to knit together into a solid lawn, pull any other weeds you find.

planting sprigs

⚐Sprigs are available by the bushel. Or you can make your own by separating grass plants from sod.

⚐Keep sprigs moist until planted. Place longer ones in furrows in prepared soil about 6 inches apart. Poke shorter pieces into the soil with your finger.

☙Sprigging is the least expensive and fastest method of establishing or repairing a lawn of warm-season grass. However, sprigs require more initial and post-planting care than plugs and are less likely to survive adverse conditions. Remember that whether you use plugs or sprigs, it is of utmost importance to keep them from drying out before you plant them.

There are three different ways to sprig a lawn. The *broadcast* method is the fastest way to install sprigs. You simply toss shredded stems evenly over a prepared, moist soil bed, then cover them with a light layer of soil. Invariably some will be completely buried and fail to grow, but the roots of most of the sprigs will take hold. The *furrow* method is more time-consuming. Dig 3-inch-deep furrows in the soil 4 to 12 inches apart. Plant each sprig so that the roots are buried and the foliage is above soil level when the furrow is smoothed over. A third option is to plant sprigs individually in a *grid pattern*.

Whichever method you choose, aftercare is critical. Walk over the area or roll it with a lawn roller at half weight to firm the soil around the crowns of the newly planted sprigs. Water immediately after planting. Continue watering frequently so the young plants don't dry out while they become established. Keep the area free of weeds. It may be necessary to fill in between the sprigs with extra soil to bring the planting bed up to grade level. This helps the horizontal runners sent out by the sprigs establish themselves quickly. When the grass is 3 inches tall, mow, cutting less than ½ inch off the blades of grass.

plugging repairs

Plugging is an ideal way to repair small sections of lawn that have died. It's also an easy way to revitalize a lawn in stages as time and money allow. The day before planting, mow the surrounding lawn area very short and water the space heavily. Plant the individual plugs 3 to 10 inches apart in a pattern that suits the empty space.

17

repairing the lawn

The best defense is to keep it healthy by fertilizing and topdressing with organic material once a year. Mow your lawn correctly and aerate it periodically to discourage thatch buildup and soil compaction. ▼Even with the best care, bare, thin, or weedy patches occasionally develop in certain areas. Deal with these problems as soon as possible so the damage doesn't spread. Weeds rapidly will fill in bare areas if you don't populate that space promptly with new grass. ▼Repairing a lawn problem is a two-step process. First, try to determine the underlying cause. Sometimes an accident, such as a fertilizer spill, creates a bare spot

YOU WILL NEED

- lawn mower
- rake
- grass seed
- seed spreader
- lawn roller (optional)
- topsoil or compost (optional)
- water

overseeding

1 Mow the existing grass as closely as possible; be careful not to scrape the crowns of the plants. Remove the clippings to expose bare soil, so the seed will have direct contact with the soil.

2 Use a garden rake to rough up the soil between the grass plants. This and the stubble of the freshly mown grass will make a good seed bed for the new seed you'll be adding.

3 Sow seed at the rate recommended for new lawns. This compensates for reduced germination as some seed falls into existing grass, not on the soil.

4 Roll the area lightly. Topdress it with topsoil or compost (optional). Water frequently. Mow the new grass when it reaches 3 inches in height.

in the lawn. Or the cause might be chronic disease, destructive insects, or competition for light and moisture from overgrown neighboring plants. Correct these deficiencies first, or your repair efforts will be futile. ❧Give a thin, tired lawn new vitality and disease resistance by overseeding it with new grass seed. In northern states, do this in the fall, so the cool-season grasses have time to develop strong roots before they have to face summer. In southern states, repair lawns of warm-weather grasses in the spring by sprigging or plugging—these grasses need warm weather to grow well.

seeding tip

Spread a thin layer of topsoil, straw, or polyspun garden fabric over the lawn area that you've just patched with seed. This protects the seed and, later, the sprouts. More importantly, by covering the soil, it reduces moisture loss. A constant supply of moisture is the key to good germination.

patching with seed

1 Delineate the spot you'll be repairing by digging all the way around its border. Remove and discard any poor grass and weeds within the area. Keep the remaining bare soil free of debris.

2 Invest as much time and effort in preparing the soil in this small repair area as you would for an entire lawn. Dig in organic matter and granular, slow-acting fertilizer. Rake the soil smooth and level.

3 Sow seed thickly. Use a variety that corresponds to the surrounding grass if possible. Otherwise use a mixture of grasses appropriate to the region.

patching with sod

Sod is the quickest and easiest way to patch a dead or damaged turf area. You can lay it any time during the season. Keep the sod moist until you plant it. Prepare the soil the same way you would for patching with seed. Keep the area an inch or so below grade so the new grass will be level with the lawn. Then cut a piece from the strip of sod to conform to the repair site. Firm it onto the soil, placing its edges snugly against the surrounding lawn. Walk on it to settle it into place. Water deeply and often.

mowing the lawn

Mowing the grass correctly improves the health and appearance of any lawn. Even older grass varieties growing in less than ideal soil respond to modern mowing practices. Your lawn will look greener, stay thicker, resist weeds more effectively, and hold up better in adverse weather with correct mowing practices that minimize the stress on grass. Mowing dramatically reduces the lawn's leaf surface, which means that the grass doesn't get as much energy from the sun to promote growth. As a result, each plant must struggle to replace its foliage as rapidly as possible so it can continue to build strong, deep roots. Constant cutting requires constant effort to

mowing height

Grass mowed with the cutting blade set high (3 to 4 inches) is healthier than grass mowed closer to the ground. Because the grass doesn't need to regrow as much leaf length, it can devote energy to growing deep roots. And the deeper the roots, the more self-reliant the grass becomes. Plants need less water and fertilizer because they get more from the soil. The resulting sturdiness helps them resist competition from nearby weeds.

Mulching mowers have specially designed blades that cut grass and leaves several times. The tiny pieces fall among the grass plants. They gradually decompose and help feed the lawn.

Riding mowers are most appropriate for large-scale, relatively flat properties and for people who are unable to walk a lot.

adjust mower height

During the growing season, you'll want to mow your lawn at different heights in response to changing weather. In spring and fall, when rainfall is most generous, most grasses do best at 2 or 2½ inches. When summer brings heat and drought, raise the mower to cut the grass at 3 inches. Longer grass suffers less stress and shades the soil, keeping it cooler and moister. The best mowers feature convenient adjustment mechanisms for raising and lowering the cutting blade. A hand-operated lever can usually be found near one or more of the wheels. On some mowers, one lever raises or lowers the four wheels at once.

replace the foliage. Therefore, it's best to mow your grass lightly, taking off about one-third of the length of the blades at a time, minimizing loss and stress. Moreover, your grass will look greener because more foliage remains. The roots grow deeper and the lawn is less vulnerable to pests and diseases. Best of all, the lawn grows more slowly. Don't cut the grass short—less than 2" tall. Tailor your mowing schedule to the type and condition of your grass. In spring and fall, when rainfall is more generous, you'll be mowing more frequently. And during the drier summers, you'll be doing so less frequently.

thatch myths debunked

Thatch isn't caused from leaving clippings on the lawn. Grass clippings are mostly water and typically break down within 10 days. Thatch is an accumulation of dead grass plant crowns and stolons that mat on the soil surface. It's usually caused by compacted soil and over-fertilization. A layer of thatch more than ¼ inch thick keeps water from reaching the soil, and it harbors pathogens. Remove it with a thatching rake or a power dethatcher.

mower heights in inches

grass	spring/fall height	summer height
cool-season grasses		
Fine fescue	2"	2½"
Tall fescue	2–2½"	3"
Kentucky bluegrass	2"	2½–3"
Perennial ryegrass	2"	2½–3"
warm-season grasses		
Bermudagrass	1½ "	2"
Buffalograss	2"	3"
Centipedegrass	1"	2"
St. Augustinegrass	1"	3"
Zoysiagrass	1–1½"	1½–2"

mowing tips

▪ **Sharpen the mower blade at least twice a season.** Dull blades increase plant stress by butchering the foliage rather than cleanly cutting it. The frayed tips turn brown, losing moisture and inviting disease.

▪ **Don't mow wet grass.** It doesn't cut evenly, and the clippings clump in the mower bell and on the turf. Walking on wet grass bruises it and spreads fungal disease to healthy grass.

▪ **Mow lightly and often.** Reduce stress on the grass plants by cutting only ⅓ of each blade with each mowing. Although this requires more frequent mowing, you're not forcing it to constantly regrow so much of its energy-collecting foliage.

▪ **Mow tall.** Tall grass shades and cools the soil, discourages weeds, and shelters beneficial ants and ground spiders that prey on pest insect eggs in the turf.

▪ **Leave the clippings.** A season's grass clippings slowly and consistently contribute as much nitrogen as a typical application of fertilizer.

▪ **Vary the mowing pattern.** Repeated walking over the same area promotes soil compaction. Prevent wear patterns by mowing horizontally one week, vertically the next, then diagonally.

21

feeding the lawn

Strictly speaking, fertilizer feeds the soil, so the soil can feed the lawn. In areas where the soil is poor, grass gets most of its nutrients from fertilizer. Grass plants are heavy feeders. They need lots of nitrogen to fuel the constant growth, necessary because the leaf blades are cut regularly during mowing. Ideally your soil will contain sufficient nitrogen (N), as well as the other essential nutrients—potassium (P) and phosphorus (K). But if it's like most soils in residential areas, it's compacted and deficient in organic matter. As a result, the soil doesn't have enough air and food to support the microbes that normally process nutrients for plants. Poor soil can't do much for the lawn besides holding the grass plants in place, so fertilizer bears most of the responsibility for grass nutrition. However, you can—over a period of years—reduce your lawn's dependency on fertilizer by periodically aerating and topdressing the soil with organic material.

❧Choosing a lawn fertilizer isn't as complicated as it may seem when walking down the aisle at the

weather

Fall is the best time to fertilize lawns of cool-weather grasses. Because grass plants are going dormant and no longer need to spend energy on foliage growth, they can devote their effort to developing strong, deep roots. For this reason, fall and winter fertilizers have a bit less nitrogen and more phosphorus.

❧To green up your lawn quickly, spray it with fast-acting, water-soluble fertilizers. The leaf tissues absorb nutrients directly, spurring rapid growth. You'll need to repeat the sprays periodically.

❧Slow-acting, granular fertilizer gives grass plants consistent, uniform nutrition for at least two or three months. It gradually releases nutrients in response to soil temperature and the activity of soil organisms.

garden center. Use a granular product to provide the annual main meal for the lawn. A complete fertilizer provides the essential nutrients (NPK) plus, in some cases, trace minerals. Although you usually can't go wrong if the bag has the words "lawn fertilizer" on it, you may prefer to determine the actual proportions of the big-three nutrients in each bag by referring to the three numbers on the label. The first number, the amount of nitrogen, is often the

highest. However, giving grass a big burst of nitrogen in spring fuels the development of foliage and stems—which means you have to mow earlier and more often. Instead, look for a continuous-acting or timed-release fertilizer that will slowly feed the lawn over the growing season. The best time to fertilize is in the fall, stimulating root growth, rather than leaf growth. Use products labeled as fall or winterizer fertilizers.

spreader tips

Use a mechanical spreader to apply granular fertilizer evenly over the lawn. Rotary or broadcast spreaders are fast and scatter the fertilizer widely. Drop spreaders release fertilizer in broad strips. To avoid missed streaks or spots with a drop spreader, make your passes in a horizontal direction first, then follow up with verticals.

23

fertilizing the natural way

The essential nutrients in some commercial fertilizers are synthesized from chemicals. Those in other fertilizers are derived from natural sources such as animal manures and pulverized rocks. Both types of formulations are available for lawns. You also can make your own lawn fertilizer from natural sources of nitrogen (N), phosphorus (P), and potassium (K). Blend roughly one pound of N with ½ pound each of P and K. Vary the ingredients for the effect you require. Sift them for uniform consistency.

sources of nitrogen	%N
dried/shredded cow manure	2
dried/shredded poultry manure	3
fish meal	5
blood meal	14
cottonseed meal	7
sources of phosphorus	**%P**
bone meal	10
rock phosphate	30
sources of potassium	**%K**
wood ashes	5
granite dust	6
greensand	7

aerating the lawn

Aeration is the best way to correct compacted soil—the number 1 enemy of healthy lawns. The soil in a typical residential yard has had all of the air pressed out of it by children's play, foot traffic, mowing, parked cars, heavy rains, and possibly construction equipment. It can't support its own life, let alone the life of grass plants. The cure is to open up the soil so air can enter it.

This enables the organisms that live on the organic matter in the soil to carry on their business of processing nutrients for plants. ▼ The best way to get air into the soil under a lawn is to make several passes with a power core-aerating machine that extracts soil cores, leaving holes that gradually fill

YOU WILL NEED

- ■ cool day
- ■ mower
- ■ water
- ■ core-aerator (power or hand model)
- ■ rake (optional)

compaction control

Choose one or more of the following options to control soil compaction under your lawn:

- •*core aeration*
- •*spiking*
- •*humic acid*
- •*organic topdressing*
- •*bioactivators*
- •*biostimulants*

1 Choose a cool day to minimize stress on the grass. Cut the lawn shorter than usual, then moisten the soil. Rent a power core-aerator to do the job in one day, or use a hand model over several days.

2 Core aerators punch hollow tines into the soil and eject plugs of soil topped by turf. Holes should be about 4 inches apart and 3 to 4 inches deep for the most effective aeration.

3 Leave the cores on the grass to dissolve gradually in the rain, providing a topdressing. The air holes fill in with moisture and organic debris.

4 Optional: Rake the small soil plugs to break them apart, accelerate decomposition, and distribute the soil evenly over the lawn.

with air, organic debris, and moisture. Aerate in spring or fall for a year or two if the soil is badly compacted. And before you overseed or install a new lawn of seed or sod, aerate to create a good soil bed. Don't roll new sod with a full-weight roller, because it will compact the soil all over again.

small-lawn hint

Hand core aerators are extremely handy for treating small lawns. Also use them for turf areas between stepping stones, along walks, and near trees to avoid damaging shallow roots.

25

aerating sandals

Special sandals with spikes allow some air to enter the soil. But they're not as effective as core aeration, because they don't remove entire cores and rarely penetrate deeply enough. However, you can use them as a stopgap measure between aerations. And if you routinely spike areas that get heavy foot traffic, you can prevent them from becoming bare.

dethatching the lawn

Thatch is an accumulation of dead crowns and stems of grass plants on the soil surface that build up around the base of living grass in the lawn. Some thatch is normal and helpful because it blocks evaporation of soil moisture. But when a layer becomes more than ¼ inch thick, it prevents water and air from entering the soil and harbors pest insects and disease pathogens. Excessive thatch usually develops if the soil is too compact or if you use too much fertilizer and pesticides. Some grass varieties, such as zoysiagrass, are more prone than others to thatch buildup. Although grass clippings accumulate on the thatch layer, preventing it from breaking down rapidly, the clippings themselves don't cause thatch. You can promote some thatch decomposition by aerating the soil and dressing it with organic material, but the fastest and most effective control method is to remove the thatch. Either rake it out of the turf by hand or remove it with a power dethatcher or a dethatching attachment on a roto-tiller. Minimize damage to the grass by doing this in the cooler seasons of spring or fall.

controlling lawn weeds

Lawn weeds are plants that aren't grass but that insist on growing in the lawn. Some may be desirable garden plants that migrate over the boundary of the flower bed. Others are unwelcome in the garden and lawn because they're coarse, ugly, and utterly lacking in charm. Whatever the case, they break up the consistent beauty of your lawn—and, worse, they overrun the grass, choking out newly emerging foliage. Weeds that produce rosettes of wide leaves close to the soil block the sun and moisture from young grass runners. The real nuisances are the weeds with deep taproots, such as dandelion and thistle, because they're so difficult to remove. ❦Weeds are often

timely weeding

Attack weeds in spring while they're young. As soon as they're visible and identifiable, dig or pull them after rain moistens the soil. Fill bare spots with grass as soon as possible, or new weeds will return with a vengeance.

turn up the heat

Some weeds, especially those that only pop up in small clusters, can be effectively killed by heat. You can pour boiling water directly on the plants, or use a propane torch to kill them.

Broadleaf plantain has 3- to 6-inch leaves that grow close to the soil. Its narrow flowers sit atop thin stalks and produce seeds June through October.

Chickweed creeps to form mats of leaves and tiny white flowers in lawns from spring through fall in most areas of the country.

Creeping Charlie snakes across lawns, forcing its way among the grass blades. It bears tiny, purple flowers amid grape-like leaves in the spring.

Dandelion produces jaunty yellow flowers emerging from low-growing rosettes of coarse-toothed leaves. Puffy seedheads assure its spread.

indicators of problems, because they move in fastest where the lawn is thin and where grass is weak and easily intimidated. They rapidly take over where soil is bare. Certain weeds signal nutritional deficiencies, compaction, and depletion of organic material. For instance, the presence of sorrel and/or dock suggest that the soil is too acid. (Most grasses prefer the soil to be slightly alkaline.) Prostrate knotweed indicates compacted soil; yellow nutsedge signals waterlogged soil. Large colonies of weeds can be the result of overusing quick-acting, water-soluble fertilizers. ◥An extra-large crop of

controlling weeds by mowing

If you mow grass at taller heights, you can do an effective job of controlling annual weeds such as crabgrass. Tall grass shades the soil where the seeds of weeds fall. If the seeds don't get sun, they don't germinate. Regular mowing discourages those that do germinate, because the mower constantly cuts off the flowers, preventing the seeds from developing. Then, when frost comes, the weeds die.

≈**Crabgrass** forms flat mats of grassy leaves in sunny lawns everywhere but Florida and the Southwest. It leaves behind copious seeds.

≈Realistically, zero tolerance for weeds in a lawn is impractical. It requires far more energy, time, and toxic herbicides than is justified or safe. Most lawns tolerate up to 20% to 30% weeds and appear green and lush. The one above has small colonies of clover, chickweed, and crabgrass that are undetectable even from a short distance.

≈ **Purslane** has succulent stems and tiny oval leaves sprawling over areas with thin, poor soil. A cousin of portulaca, it produces tiny, yellow flowers.

controlling lawn weeds (cont'd.)

weeds also may be a signal of incorrect mowing. If you mow the grass too short, you reduce its vigor and inhibit its ability to shade the soil and keep weed seeds from germinating. Crabgrass, clover, and chickweed thrive in short grass. ❧It's neither necessary nor practical to eradicate all weeds in your lawn. Your goal should be to control their numbers so that the weeds don't detract from your lawn's appearance. The best way to control weeds over the long term is to correct any soil problems and adopt good maintenance practices to keep the lawn dense and healthy. Pulling out emerging weeds early in the season is the simplest immediate control. This keeps annual weeds from setting seed before they die. It's easier to pull out perennial weeds when they're

controlling annual weeds

Apply pre-emergents to control annual weeds before they sprout. An environmentally friendly treatment, made of corn gluten, is best applied in the fall. Most chemical pre-emergents, however, are best applied in early spring, before the forsythia are in full bloom. They form a chemical barrier on the grass that inhibits germination of all seeds. Don't aerate or overseed grass treated with conventional pre-emergents until fall.

Veronica forms tight mats of leaf-covered stems on the soil. The small, bright blue flowers of this self-sowing annual bloom from April to August.

Violets are perennial garden plants that tend to seed into lawns. Lavender or white flowers on thin stems poke above heart-shaped leaves in spring.

White clover features small balls of tiny, white flowers on thin stalks. They rise above three-petaled leaves that sprawl as a mat of rambling stems.

Wood sorrel, or oxalis, forms creeping mats or small upright plants bearing small, green or bronze clover-shaped leaves and tiny, yellow flowers.

young. ¶If weeds become well established in your lawn, choose the least toxic herbicide. Spot-treat isolated patches of weeds with a spritz of herbicide. Spray or spread herbicide over your entire lawn only if weeds are extensively distributed throughout the turf. Because the weeds are growing among plants you don't want to kill—the grass—use a selective herbicide. You can buy one for *grassy* weeds, such as nutsedge, another for *broadleaf* weeds such as plantain. After the weeds die, clear out the remnants and immediately scatter grass seed or lay sod on the bare spots.

edible lawn weeds

plant	edible part	use/preparation
Burdock	root	pickled, boiled in soups and stews
Chickweed	leaves	chopped in salads
Cresses	leaves	young in salad; cooked in soup
Dandelion	leaves, flowers	young leaves in salads, steamed, wilted, or cooked in dandelion gravy (served over mashed potatoes); young flowers in wine; dipped in egg then cornmeal and fried
Lamb's-quarter	leaves, shoots	young in salad; cook and use like spinach
Plantain	leaves	blanch and saute in butter and garlic
Purslane	leaves, stems	very young leaves chopped in salads, salty garnish; blanch and saute with olive oil, garlic, and chile
Red clover	flowers	chopped in salads, steeped in tea, cooked in soup
Shepherd's purse	leaves	blanch and saute with olive oil, garlic, and chile
Violet	leaves, flowers	young leaves in salad, add to marinara sauce; flowers in fruit salad, syrup, sorbet, candied

controlling lawn pests

Some pest insects are always present in a lawn. Usually they only use it for a time to shelter their eggs and feed their larvae. The adult beetles and moths are an integral part of the richly varied assortment of living organisms that inhabit residential ecosystems. In their various life stages, they remain inconspicuous most of the time while they play their role in maintaining balance, seldom causing visible damage. However, something unusual—such as a significant decline in the health of the lawn, extremes in temperature or rainfall, or the destruction of the pests' natural predators—occasionally takes place. The result is an explosion of the pest population—and visible lawn

using birds to control pests

Birds nesting in or around your property eat an enormous number of insects. Even those species that normally eat seeds and fruits will seek out insects for their insatiable young ones who can't yet digest seeds. Offer their mom and dad some water, shelter, and feeder snacks to keep them nearby.

army worm

description and trouble signs

These caterpillars cluster to feed on grass leaves at night and rest under dead or dying sod during the daytime. Their bodies are brown and hairy, and they have green, beige, or black stripes down their backs. In spring, adult moths deposit eggs on the grass, where the newly hatched larvae begin to feed. Army worms are most active in the spring and fall, and you usually can spot their handiwork in the form of irregular bare patches in the turf.

controls

- Spray *Bacillus thurengiensis* (Bt) on the affected grass during the period when the army worms are feeding. Repeat every 10 to 14 days until they're gone. Reapply if it rains.
- Spray beneficial (predatory) nematodes on affected lawn areas as directed on the product label.

billbug

description and trouble signs

Adult billbugs chew holes in grass stems to deposit eggs in them. The reddish-brown beetles are ¾ inch long and have long snouts. Newly hatched, legless larvae feed on grass stems and crowns, breaking them off at the soil line and creating patches of dead grass. Sometimes the white, pudgy larvae are visible on driveways in May or June. Damage appears mid-June through July. They work quickly and are particularly fond of Kentucky bluegrass.

controls

- Remove the thatch layer to expose the billbugs to their bird and insect predators.
- Drench the affected area of lawn with insecticidal soap and water as directed on the package label.
- Spray heavily infested lawns with a commercial broad-spectrum insecticide listed for billbugs.

damage. ❧A good offense is the best defense, and prevention is the best way to deal with lawn pests. Head off potential problems by taking measures to maintain the natural balance in the yard and create a stable environment that will support and maintain a healthy lawn. Grow several kinds of plants in addition to grass to ensure the presence of a variety of beneficial insects. Avoid using broad-spectrum insecticides that are indiscriminate—killing good bugs as well as the bad ones. Put up feeders, birdbaths, and nesting boxes to encourage birds to stay nearby and patrol for pest insects. Plant varieties

Using Bt

Bt (Bacillus thurengiensis) *is the active ingredient in many caterpillar insecticides. This bacteria paralyzes the caterpillars' digestive tracts when they eat it, causing the caterpillars to die from starvation. Before applying Bt, mow the lawn. Then mix the powder with water as directed on the package. You can add a surfactant or sticker such as a couple of drops of liquid soap—the plainer the better—to help the solution adhere to grass leaves and penetrate thatch. Spray leaf surfaces until the blades are dripping. Bt breaks down faster in sunlight, so spray on a cloudy day.*

31

chinch bug

description and trouble signs
Tiny, inconspicuous bugs damage grass in each of their life stages. Adults have black bodies marked with a dark, triangular pad separating their folded wings. Immature bugs are reddish-colored. They're happiest in hot, dry weather and create large, yellowish, spreading circular patches in lawns that are afflicted with thatch. Chinch bugs often begin near sidewalks and streets, congregating at the center of these areas as the grass there turns brown and dies.

controls
- Remove the thatch layer to expose the chinch bugs to their bird and insect predators.
- Drench the affected area of lawn with insecticidal soap and water as directed on the package label.
- Spray heavily infested lawns with a commercial broad-spectrum insecticide listed for chinch bugs.

spider mite

description and trouble signs
Various mites afflict lawn grasses (and weeds) by sucking juices from the undersides of the leaves, causing them to yellow, wilt, and die. Mites are most active during the hot months of summer, especially when there is little rain or irrigation. Although they're virtually impossible to see without magnification, their trademark fine webbing is often visible between leaves. Typical examples are clover mites, which are red, and Bermudagrass mites, which are greenish.

controls
- Water the lawn to eliminate the dry environment that mites prefer.
- Suspend fertilizing to limit the amount of succulent grass growth that attracts mites.
- Drench the affected area of lawn with insecticidal soap and water as directed on the package label.

controlling lawn pests (cont'd.)

of grass that are resistant to pests in your region. ❧Mow the grass tall to shelter beneficial ants and spiders that reduce the number of pests by eating their eggs. Aerate and feed the lawn to help it develop deep roots so it can withstand the stress of minor insect damage. Be observant. Watch for trouble signs such as mole activity, flocks of starlings or other birds on the lawn, and moths flying low over the turf. ❧In spite of your best efforts, however, extreme weather or other circumstances occasionally can upset the delicate balance, enabling pest insects to get an upper hand. At this point, you need to take action. But first, determine how much damage you really have—and whether you can live with it. ❧Several weapons are effective against common pests. Spray

routine timing of pests

The emergence of pest insects is amazingly predictable. Their arrival is usually within a day or two of the same date, year after year. This makes control much easier because you can begin your measures immediately, before populations expand. Prevent problems next year by picking as many beetles as possible off plants before they can lay their eggs. And write in your garden journal or calendar the date they emerge this year, and mark that date on next year's calendar so you can be alert for them.

cutworm

description and trouble signs

Cutworm describes many kinds of moths whose larvae plague lawns. The caterpillars are fat, soft, and bristly, and their color depends on the adult moth species. Variegated cutworms are gray, mottled with dark brown and have a row of colorful spots running down their backs. They live at the soil surface and are most active from spring through late summer. Cutworms leave telltale dead spots where they have cut the grass stems at their base.

controls
- Drench (puddle) affected areas of the lawn with water to force the worms to the surface. Then you can handpick and collect them for the trash.
- Spray Bt on the grass when cutworms are feeding.
- Spray beneficial (predatory) nematodes on the affected parts of the lawn.

mole cricket

description and trouble signs

These brown, 1½-inch-long insects chew the stems of warm-season grasses above and below the soil surface. They're partial to moist, warm weather in the South. Mole crickets work night and day, creating areas of the lawn that appear streaked or closely clipped. Underneath, their travels create tunnels 6 to 8 inches deep, damaging grass roots. The air spaces cause the roots to dry out and the turf above to feel spongy.

controls
- Remove the thatch layer to discourage crickets.
- Spray beneficial nematodes on the grass.
- Drench the affected area with insecticidal soap.
- Spray the lawn with an insecticide containing neem, as directed on its label.
- Sprinkle diatomaceous earth (DE) on affected areas.

the grass with insecticidal soap or drench the soil where soft-bodied pests are active. Or coat the blades of grass with the bacteria, *Bacillus thurengiensis* (Bt), which sickens and kills various caterpillars when they eat it. You can spray the lawn with microscopic predatory nematodes that burrow into the soil and seek out caterpillars as hosts for their eggs. The new larvae kill the caterpillars. Handpick or trap moths and beetles to reduce the egg population. If these methods don't work, your local Cooperative Extension service or garden center can recommend a chemical control.

friendly ants

Though ants are absolute nuisances in the kitchen, they're allies in your yard. They range through the soil, preying on the eggs of numerous pest insects and, as a result, significantly reduce their populations. Normally they nest at the edges of lawns, in stone walls, or in crevices. Mounded nests all over the lawn indicate soil problems such as a deficiency of organic matter.

33

sod webworm

description and trouble signs
Various moths lay eggs that hatch into grass-eating caterpillars. They vary from greenish to beige to brown or gray and have shiny brown heads and four parallel rows of distinctive dark spots on their backs. They build silk-lined cocoons on thatch, where they lurk and feed on grass blades. Kentucky bluegrass and fine fescues are among their favorites. They cause small brown spots in a lawn in late spring, which become large dead patches by midsummer.

controls
- Remove the thatch layer to deny sod webworms a place to lay eggs.
- Spray beneficial nematodes on the grass.
- Drench the affected area with insecticidal soap.
- Spray Bt on the grass when the sod webworms are feeding.

white grub

description and trouble signs
These beetle larvae are thick, white worms with brown heads. They lie curled in the soil and, as the weather warms, migrate to the surface to feed on grass roots. They emerge in summer as Japanese beetles, June bugs, and others. Grubs typically do their damage by destroying grass roots, causing irregular brown patches of lawn. At this point, you can pull up the sod easily, revealing the perpetrators in the soil beneath.

controls
- Aerate or spike the lawn in late spring to kill the grubs that are near the soil surface.
- Spray beneficial nematodes on the grass.
- Mow grass tall in summer after the beetles emerge.
- Collect the adult beetles as they feed on favorite plants before they can lay eggs in the lawn.

controlling lawn diseases

Most lawn diseases are caused by fungus.
Because of this, the methods of prevention and control are pretty much the same. Fungal spores continually exist in grass, thatch, and soil. Other organisms that share the same living quarters maintain the balance of these populations of fungus by preying on them. Occasionally, fungus outbreaks occur when weather or conditions in the lawn change, upsetting the balance. Then the fungi overrun their predators and overwhelm the nearby grass. Usually the first signs of trouble are discolored patches in the lawn. To verify that the problem is a disease—and not insect infestation—try to pull up a handful of grass plants. If the grass

weather

Fungal disease outbreaks are often caused by temporary weather extremes. Certain diseases become active when the weather suddenly gets very hot and dry; others respond to unusually cool and moist conditions. When this happens, the infection is usually temporary. The best response may be simply to wait until the extremes moderate. However, if a disease appears chronically, regardless of weather, you'll need to take control measures.

Brownspot causes sizable, brownish gray, irregular patches, sometimes ringing circular green spots, during hot, humid days of mid- to late summer. It likes grass stressed by overfertilization and thatch.

Dollar spot thrives in humid weather on dry, undernourished lawns. It appears as bleached beige spots of dead grass up to 5 inches in diameter that may be covered with cobwebs in early morning.

Fusarium blight thrives in hot, humid areas and starts as 2- to 6-inch reddish spots that turn tan then yellow. Roots and crowns show rot.

Leaf spot causes pale-centered, blackish purple oval spots on damp grass—mainly in early spring or late fall—on shady, closely mowed lawns.

doesn't come out easily, the problem probably is caused by disease. ❧It is easy to prevent many diseases before they take hold. Choose modern, resistant varieties of grass. Plant a mixture of many kinds of grass so their vulnerabilities offset one another. Minimize stress: Mow the lawn high, use restraint with fertilizer, and water well—only when necessary—to encourage deep roots. Aerate the soil periodically and remove excessive thatch. ❧Resort to control measures only if infection is serious or chronic. Protect nearby healthy turf from infection by spraying it with a fungicide formulated for grass.

controlling stress

Grass that is stressed is most vulnerable to disease. Some stress, such as that caused by atypical weather, is uncontrollable. However, you can avoid stress caused by:

- *too much or too little fertilizer*
- *overly acidic soil*
- *insufficient sunlight*
- *excessively short grass*
- *heavy thatch*
- *lack of water*
- *compacted soil*

Fairy ring infection causes bright-green, circular patches of fast-growing grass in the Pacific Northwest. Perimeters brown, the grass declines, and a cluster of mushrooms may appear at the edges.

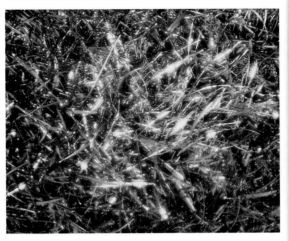

Pythium blight starts as blackened, water-soaked, 2-inch patches that eventually lie flat. In humid weather, a cottony growth may be visible. Foot traffic spreads the disease, but dry weather stops it.

Powdery mildew coats Kentucky bluegrass with a grayish film in cool, humid, shaded areas. Severe infection turns grass yellow and kills it.

Red thread, a problem in the Northeast and Pacific Northwest, creates rusty red lawn patches. Cool, humid weather and low nitrogen encourage it.

regional lawn-care checklist

Cool Climates

Spring

- ☐ Sharpen the lawn mower blade if you didn't do so during the winter.
- ☐ Have the lawn mower serviced.
- ☐ Patch or overseed early with perennial ryegrass. Its rapid germination ensures sturdier seedlings going into summer.
- ☐ Aerate the lawn to treat compacted soil.
- ☐ Topdress the lawn with organic matter, if necessary.
- ☐ Spread granular, slow-acting fertilizer. (This is optional if you fertilized in the fall or winter.)

Summer

- ☐ When hot weather sets in, raise the mower to cut at 3 inches or higher.
- ☐ If the soil is good, water only when rainfall is delayed more than 10 to 14 days.
- ☐ If the soil is poor and rain is scarce, water weekly.
- ☐ Spot-treat weeds and patch bare spots.
- ☐ Halfway through the season, sharpen the lawn-mower blade.

Warm Climates

Spring

- ☐ Plug, sprig, or sod new lawns after you've carefully prepared the soil.
- ☐ Sharpen the lawn-mower blade.
- ☐ Fertilize lawns for spring greenup. If soil is acidic, do not lime until fall.
- ☐ Dethatch and aerate the lawn, if necessary.

Summer

- ☐ For summer mowing, adjust mower to correct height for the type of grass in your lawn.
- ☐ Water lawn as needed—frequently if the soil is poor, every 7 to 10 days if the soil is good.
- ☐ Use plugs or sprigs to patch any bare spots in the lawn where weeds once grew or insects caused damage.

Fall

- ❏ If soil is too acid, spread lime. (Wait at least two weeks to fertilize.)
- ❏ Aerate compacted soil under turf, if you didn't do so in the spring.
- ❏ Topdress with organic material or mow a layer of fallen leaves to mulch them into the lawn.
- ❏ Just after Labor Day, seed or sod new lawns, or overseed existing ones.
- ❏ Fertilize the lawn on or about Thanksgiving to promote strong root growth throughout the winter.
- ❏ Prevent the grass from matting under the snow by lowering the mower and cutting the grass a bit shorter just before winter.

Winter

- ❏ Put out markers to indicate lawn edges so you don't damage the lawn when you shovel snow.
- ❏ Avoid walking on frosted or snow-covered lawns.
- ❏ Drain gas from lawn mowers and weed trimmers.
- ❏ Purchase and use non-salt de-icer for sidewalks and drives.

- ❏ Overseed warm-weather grasses with annual rye to produce a green turf during the winter.
- ❏ Sharpen the lawn-mower blade again to help keep the grass healthy.
- ❏ Use plugs or sprigs to patch any bare spots in lawn where weeds once grew or insects caused damage.

- ❏ Mow lawn if you overseeded it with ryegrass.
- ❏ Install sprinkler system if turf is planted in sandy soil. (This is optional, depending on your watering habits.)
- ❏ Service power lawn mower and weed trimmer.

lawn alternatives

choosing a groundcover

All kinds of plants make good groundcovers.
In spite of this, lawn grass continues to be what most Americans use to cover large expanses of the yard and to keep it from washing away. But there are lots of other groundcovers —shrubs, vines, annuals, perennials, conifers, and herbs—that do a better job of protecting soil and decorating yards. Almost all of them require less overall attention, including watering, fertilizing, mowing, and repairing. And almost all of them are more versatile and contribute more to a healthy environment than grass. ¶The universal stereotype of plain-green, low-growing plants doesn't define a groundcover plant. Even though the familiar and

season hint

Many good groundcover plants are annuals or herbaceous (soft-stemmed) perennials which die back in the winter. The soil they protected all summer becomes bare and is exposed to harsh winter weather. To keep the soil in good condition, spread 3 to 4 inches of organic material over the area after the ground freezes.

Barrenwort is a perennial that blooms in spring. After its dainty yellow, pink, or white flowers fade, the wiry stems keep the heart-shaped leaves until fall. Grows in partial shade. Zones 5–9.

Bishop's weed, or goutweed, spreads readily. Its leaves are plain green or variegated, and they serve well in sun or shade, long after their white flowers fade in early summer. Zones 4–9.

Cotoneaster is a hardy shrub. This low-growing, tiny-leafed version bears small flowers in spring and red berries in fall. It handles dry slopes. Zones 5–7.

Heath and Heather are low-growing plants that accept sun or shade. They bear tiny flower spikes in spring (heath) or fall (heather). Zones 5–7.

reliable pachysandra and English ivy do an excellent job of protecting and beautifying areas—large and small—lots of other plants do just as well. Actually, any mass planting that grows together to form a canopy and effectively covers the soil with texture and color is a potential groundcover. There are no rules for height or type, though in some cases you may want something that remains low to the ground or, conversely, is tall enough to hide eyesores.

The site will be a major factor in your choices. For example, some plants thrive in shady areas, while others function better on slopes or in long borders.

Bugleweed, or ajuga, grows whorls of purple-tinged, green, or variegated leaves where its runners root. It bears spikes of blue, pink, or white flowers in spring. The plant is easy to control. Zones 3–9.

Cinnamon fern grows in shady areas. It has a cloud of soft green foliage and forms vase-shaped clumps of fronds, punctuated with cinnamon-brown reproductive stems. It spreads slowly. Zones 4–8.

Hosta foliage has varied colors, patterns, and shapes to brighten shady areas all season. In summer, it bears white or lavender flowers. Zones 3–8.

Irish moss, or baby tears, forms a tight mat of tiny, hairy, green leaves and blooms in summer. It grows in moist, shady areas in zones 10 and 11.

choosing a groundcover (cont'd.)

You can use all kinds of garden standbys as groundcovers, or look to new plants at the nursery. Consider using culinary herbs, ornamental grasses, or the newer low-maintenance roses. Imagine patches of ferns, spring bulbs, or mosses. Groundcover plants shelter the soil and the living organisms that dwell in and around it. Groundcovers serve as a living mulch to reduce moisture evaporation, control erosion, and prevent harsh weather from compacting the soil. Use a variety of plants on different parts of your property. Diversity not only makes your outdoor environment more attractive, but it also creates a healthier ecosystem. A

mixing bulbs and evergreens

Hardy flowering bulbs cover the ground spectacularly in spring. However, after they bloom and their leaves mature and die back, the ground is bare. Take advantage of the beauty of these flowering bulbs—and maintain a year-round covering on the soil—by planting them among evergreen groundcover plants such as pachysandra, ivy, or even a ground-hugging juniper. The green foliage sets off the colorful bulbs, then hides the ripening leaves afterward.

Ivy, a classic groundcover, has tough, triangular, evergreen leaves on strong, running stems. Leaves may be 1 to 4 inches wide, variegated in cream, white, gray, and green. Zones 5–10.

Wild ginger clusters in neat, low patches of patterned leaves. Its heart-shaped leaves hide inconspicuous flowers in spring. It spreads slowly in shady sites. Highly collectible. Zones 2–8.

Lungwort likes moist soil in partial shade. It's available in a host of variegated white and green leaf patterns and shapes. Tiny, funnel-shaped spring flowers begin pink and fade to purplish. Zones 4–8.

Maidenhair fern features dark, 2-foot stalks, branched into a curved, horizontal pattern covered with dainty, pale green leaflets. It spreads slowly in shady, cool, moist soil in zones 3–8.

broad selection of plants attracts a wider range of beneficial insects and other creatures to control pests and diseases. Include a few plants that are indigenous to your region, because they're particularly adapted to your climate and soil. They also serve wildlife better than others and are typically very low-maintenance. Use groundcovers to solve landscape problems around the yard. They'll cover surface tree roots, brighten shady spots, and hide eyesores such as decaying stumps and utility boxes.

Lady's mantle spreads its beauty in sun or partial shade. In late spring, clusters of tiny chartreuse flowers atop long stems emerge from distinctive, gray-green, scalloped leaves. Zones 4–7.

Lily-of-the-valley spreads in shady areas by means of underground bulblets. Its legendary fragrant flowers bloom in spring. Like other hardy bulbs, its leaves die back by late summer. Zones 2–7.

Prickly pear cactus thrives in any soil. Waxy, yellow, cupped flowers appear at the top margins of its rounded, prickly, succulent leaves in summer, followed by edible fruit. Zones 6–8.

Periwinkle, also known as myrtle, is low-growing, with small, narrowly oval, glossy green leaves all year long. Small, blue flowers decorate the mass of foliage in the spring. Zones 6–8.

choosing a groundcover (cont'd.)

Plants with thorns or stickers discourage trespassers from cutting across certain areas. ❦In large yards, you'll get the best effect by planting smaller, finer-textured plants in the foreground and locating taller, coarser-textured ones toward the back. Use brightly colored varieties to draw attention to an area or divert it from another one. Switch from one plant to another to indicate boundary changes.

❦You can find potential groundcover plants for almost every landscape. Some prefer shady, moist conditions, while others can handle dry or sunny sites and poor soil. The virtue of most groundcover plants is that they're inclined to grow larger in

using shrubs as groundcovers

Shrubs make excellent groundcovers. Ground-hugging or dwarf versions of evergreens, such as juniper—or small, low-growers, such as wintercreeper or cotoneaster—are ideal for sunny slopes or other areas that are difficult or dangerous to mow or where erosion is a problem. You can even cover that sunny slope with roses. New, low-maintenance landscape roses, such as Flower Carpet®, Meidiland™, or 'The Fairy,' bloom all season with virtually no care.

Sedums have succulent leaves on straight, 2-foot stems. Rounded flowerheads mature over the season from pale green, to fuzzy pink, to red, to rust—then dry for winter beauty. Zones 4–9.

Snow-in-summer is very easy to grow and enthusiastically creeps over sunny sites with poor soil. In June and July, its silver-gray leaves are covered with small white flowers. Zones 3–7.

Sweet woodruff weaves a web of fine roots just under the soil. Whorls of leaves are topped by delicate, white spring flowers. Plants are tenacious, neat, and tidy. Zones 5–8.

Thyme offers a selection of low-growing, woody, evergreen plants. Most have small, dark green or variegated aromatic leaves. Tiny, lavender-pink flowers appear in late spring. Zones 4–9.

clumps or by running stems or roots. As a result, their areas are filled with vigorous spreaders. However, beware of those that are so aggressive that they need constant controlling. They endanger other plants and create more problems than they solve.

Spotted dead nettle sports crinkled, variegated leaves on 6-inch stems. It likes shade and produces tiny, lavender flowers intermittently over the summer if left unsheared. Zones 4–8.

Variegated lilyturf (liriope) forms neat clumps of 8- to 12-inch, straplike leaves, striped yellow and green. Tiny lavender flowers appear on spikes in late summer. It grows in sun or shade in zones 6–10.

planting a groundcover

1 Purchase flats of rooted cuttings or individual young plants, or use divisions from existing plants. Keep their roots moist. Dig organic matter and slow-acting fertilizer into the soil.

2 Set the small, rooted plants in a grid pattern, equidistant from one another. The closer together you plant them, the sooner they'll knit together to cover the soil and create a continuous mass.

3 Water the transplants well and mulch between them with organic material. This will keep the soil moist longer and discourage weeds until the transplants have enough time to grow together.

groundcover buying guide

You'll find that the most satisfactory groundcovers will have many of these qualities:

- *Spread fairly quickly to cover bare soil.*
- *Tolerate a range of soil types.*
- *Spread reliably, but not rampantly.*
- *Easy to pull up if they spread too far.*
- *Have winter interest such as evergreen leaves, berries, or seedheads.*
- *Have interesting shapes and colors.*
- *Need minimal pruning, mowing, or grooming.*
- *Hold up for many years with little or no fuss.*

ornamental grasses

Ornamental grasses are easy to grow. As a group, they're tough and self-reliant, needing very little care over the years. Although they are members of the same family as the lawn grasses, they couldn't be more different. In fact, they have a host of virtues that lawn grasses lack. For starters, ornamental grasses boast resistance to drought, pests, and disease. They offer seasonal color, variegated leaves, and showy flowers. These strong characteristics make them a truly low-maintenance, high-performance group of plants. They're also environmentally correct— requiring no fertilizers, pesticides, or additional watering. Furthermore, they continue to perform all

weather

Although ornamental grasses tend to be stiff and sturdy, some of the tall ones are vulnerable to heavy winds and rainstorms. They're more likely to get matted down if they're not getting as much sun as they would like. Use unobtrusive stakes and string supports to keep the stems from flopping.

Blue fescue grows as 12-inch-wide clumps, 6 to 12 inches tall. It flowers in the summer in response to the heat. Its distinctive gray blue leaf blades are a standout in the winter. Zones 4–8.

Maiden grass (miscanthus) has many popular varieties, developing clumps of widely arching, 1-inch-wide, pointed leaves, reaching up to 12 feet tall in various colorations. Zones 5–9.

Hakone grass can handle shade. It forms low, arching clumps of bamboolike, variegated leaves. This grass also does well in containers. Zones 5–9.

Pampas grass has tall, plumed stems that are often used in dried floral crafts. It grows best where summers are hot and dry. Zones 7–10.

winter, creating light and movement with their handsome, vertical, straw-colored leaves and fluffy seedheads. Perhaps part of their appeal lies in the ancestral relationship we have with them. From the grassy savannas of Africa to the Great Prairie of North America, people lived among tall grasses. They built their homes with them and fed their livestock with them. ❧Like lawn grasses, some ornamentals adapt to cool weather, others to warm conditions. Some spread by widening clumps, while others send runners or horizontal roots under the soil. And, like their cousins, they come in annual and perennial

dividing grasses

Divide overlarge clumps of ornamental grass in spring before the new shoots start to appear. Cut back the dried, bleached stems and then dig up the rootball. Use a sharp spade, saw, or ax to hack rooted chunks from the rootball, then replant each one. If the rootball is too large to dig up, cut out pie-shaped wedges while it's in the ground. Remove them to replant elsewhere, and fill in their spots with soil.

47

🌾**Eulalia grass** is beautiful in winter. Its September flowers release seeds and dry atop bleached, dried, grass fronds. Use it to shelter and feed birds and screen out noise or neighbors. Zones 5-9.

other great grasses

There are many wonderful grasses suitable for residential yards and gardens. In addition to the ones individually pictured and described here, many others have similar virtues. Some are annual, others perennial. They offer a variety of sizes and colors, as well as interesting flowers.

name	height
Big bluestem/Andropogon	5–8 feet
Feathertop	1½–2½ feet
Feather reed grass	Up to 5 feet
Giant reed	14–18 feet
Japanese blood grass	1–1½ feet
Little bluestem	2–3 feet
Meadow foxtail	2–3 feet
Northern sea grass (oat grass)	3–4 feet
Ravenna grass	7–15 feet
Switch grass	Up to 7 feet

🌾**Purple maiden grass** flowers earlier than most, its pink tint evolving to outstanding red-orange fall foliage. Water in drought. Zones 5–9.

ornamental grasses (cont'd.)

varieties. But the similarity ends there. Ornamental grasses have enormous versatility. They not only make good groundcovers, but they also can play lots of other roles in your yard. Include them in flower beds and borders as vertical accents and color contrasts. Use low-growers to cascade over walls, and substitute taller versions for shrubs. Grow grasses in containers. Use them as accents. Plant them along boundaries as a living fence, or use them to screen a view and buffer traffic noise. Bring them indoors, too, and use their wonderful seedheads in dried and fresh flower arrangements or floral crafts. Although most ornamental grasses thrive in

using grasses as groundcovers

Ornamental grasses make excellent, long-lasting groundcovers. Because they generally require very little maintenance, they're a good choice for sunny sites. Choose those that develop as clumps that gradually enlarge each year to fill in and cover bare ground. Avoid those that spread by underground roots, because they're often hard to control.

Ribbon grass features creamy stripes on its spiky-green leaves. Because it spreads vigorously by underground runners, it eventually becomes difficult to control. Try planting it in a container. Zones 4–9.

Purple fountain grass is known for its upright, purplish red foliage and soft, fuzzy flowers atop 2- to 3-foot stems in summer. Drought-tolerant and hardy in Zone 9, it's often grown as an annual.

Fescue 'Elijah Blue' is a popular form of blue fescue with a strong, silvery blue color that grows to 8 inches tall. It has a tough constitution. Plant it in a sunny site that has well-drained soil. Zones 4–8.

Zebra grass is a form of maiden grass that grows in narrow clumps and is more floppy than upright. Its trademark foliage features horizontal yellow stripes against a green background. Zones 4–9.

hot sun and ordinary soil, some tolerate partial shade and moist soil. Choose grasses that suit the site. Plant in the spring at the exact depth as they were in their pots. Water well until they get established and send up new shoots. Don't fertilize or add any amendments, such as peat moss, to the soil. The only attention they require is cutting back in spring to make way for new shoots. After a few years, the clump may outgrow its allotted space. Move it or dig it up and divide it in the spring.

A garden full of ornamental grasses is a special place of color and movement all year long. First, the various grasses display their uniquely colored and patterned leaves. Then their flowers bloom, release seeds, and become puffy and delicate, as the grasses bleach and dry to a golden, winter beige.

A planting of five types of maiden grasses by a pool adds to the color, quiet, and privacy of the scene. The tall, softly arching leaves soften the effect of the adjoining masonry by suggesting falling water. The grasses also absorb sound and screen the view to enclose the pool area.

planting a slope

can be problem areas. Sometimes they're so steep that you have trouble keeping your footing while working there. And they tend to erode unless they are planted to stabilize and hold the soil. Although your first thought may be to plant grass, the same grasses that make a great lawn aren't suitable for most slopes. Gentle inclines are difficult to mow and maintain. Steep ones are so dangerous that lawn mower manufacturers warn against mowing them. The best solution in either case is to plant low-maintenance plants as a groundcover. Soil on slopes tends to be dry because water runs downward before it has a chance to soak in. South-facing slopes are the toughest, because they receive intense sun during a good portion of the day—in summer and winter. As

YOU WILL NEED

- gloves
- weeding tools
- boards, stakes, hammer
- shovel and trowel
- organic material
- slow-acting fertilizer
- garden rake
- plants
- mulch or netting

1 Clear the area of weeds, stones, and any other debris. Wear a thick pair of gloves to protect your hands from glass or other sharp objects.

2 Save extra work later by taking the time now to pull or kill roots of perennial weeds. They'll be harder to deal with after the groundcover is established.

5 Plant as close together as the supply of plants allows, so they'll grow together faster. Stagger the rows so the plants can hold the soil better.

6 Cover the planting with polyspun garden fabric, landscape fabric, bark nuggets, or straw to hold the soil when it rains. Netting also works well.

a result, plants on these slopes are subject to scorching and desiccation. Fortunately, several alternatives, such as ornamental grasses, artemisias, juniper, and rosemary, can stand up to these pressures and stay attractive year-round. ❦Prepare, water, and mulch the soil on a slope just as you would anywhere else you'd be planting groundcovers. However, you'll want to cover the soil on a grade as fast as possible, because once you've cleaned it off for planting, it's vulnerable to erosion. So spend the money it takes to get larger plants with well-developed root systems that will spread quickly. Then plant them as closely as possible so they will blend together rapidly and anchor the soil.

planting shrubs as groundcovers

Before you plant shrubs as groundcovers, kill the weeds in the area with a natural herbicide. Then dig individual holes, exactly as deep as each plant rootball is tall. Set each plant in a hole upright, then fill in and firm the soil over the roots. Water, then mulch the entire area with some coarse organic material to hold the soil until the plants spread to cover it.

51

3 Prepare for possible erosion after the slope is exposed by setting up a temporary barrier to retain the soil while you're planting.

4 If the soil is compacted and infertile, dig in some organic matter (to improve drainage and water retention) and some granular, slow-acting fertilizer.

choosing a vine

By their nature, vines are upwardly mobile. They insist on vertical progress, even though they're firmly rooted in the soil. This virtue makes them enormously useful in residential yards. Their lush leaves and, more often than not, appealing flowers decorate the landscape with pillars, arches, and swags of color and texture. Many provide late-season bonuses of decorative seedpods, edible or ornamental fruit, and colorful fall foliage. And there's fragrance from moonflowers, autumn clematis, and others. ❦Some vines, such as morning glory and hyacinth bean, are annuals. They die at the first hard frost in fall, so you'll have to plant them anew each spring—although some self-seed

weather

Vines moderate temperature. When their leaves cover a masonry wall in the summer, they block the glare of the sun and its reflected heat, cooling the area. Then when deciduous vines drop their leaves in the fall, the exposed wall absorbs heat and reflects light to create a warmer microclimate during the winter.

Boston ivy is a clinger that drapes walls with shiny, three-lobed leaves in summer. In fall, they turn deep red, and the reddish stems sport dark berries that birds love. Zones 4–8.

Bougainvillea flowers are tiny and white, upstaged by the brightly colored papery bracts that surround them. It's a southern staple along fences and on arbors and is hardy only in Zone 10.

Climbing hydrangea takes a few years to establish. Early each summer, its 6- to 8-inch-wide, lacy white blooms are worth the wait. Zones 4–8.

Dutchman's pipe is named for the unusually shaped flowers that nestle among drapes of foot-long green leaves. It's hardy to Zone 4 and grows in shade.

and save you the trouble. The woody vines are perennials. Kiwi, wisteria, climbing hydrangea, and wintercreeper are basically vertically inclined shrubs. They grow more substantial each year, the stems thickening with age, and require the same type of care as earthbound shrubs. Vines are ideal for small properties. Because they occupy a very small area of soil, spreading upward instead of outward, they use planting space efficiently.

Vines provide a link between the earth and the sky. They're especially useful in areas where trees are scarce, serving as substitutes by creating their own

Clematis flowers are summer standouts in purple, white, and shades of pink. This perennial's seedheads are composed of curved filaments that beautify through fall. Clematis is hardy to Zone 5.

Hardy kiwi produces 2- to 3-inch green leaves that shelter inconspicuous flowers. They give way to edible, inch-long, greenish fruits. Hardy to Zone 4.

dangerous vine

Certain vines are not welcome in home landscapes. Some are health hazards. For instance, every part of the poison ivy vine contains a toxic resin that causes severe contact dermatitis. Others are simply too aggressive. While you may be able to use constant pruning to control vines, such as Oriental bittersweet, porcelainberry, wild grape, and kudzu (above), it's impossible to prevent their escape into the wild—birds carry their seeds into parks, roadsides, woodlands, and fields. There they run rampant, choking out natural vegetation and smothering trees.

choosing a vine (cont'd.)

kind of shade and balance in the landscape. ¶Place vines strategically along boundaries or over walls and fences to define a space. Drape them on arbors or along railings to line passageways and guide foot traffic. Create a special rest and contemplation space around a vine-covered garden seat. Plant vines with drop-dead gorgeous flowers, such as clematis or mandevilla, to climb the mailbox post out front. Or use others to anchor large garden beds and balance their proportions. ¶Vines also link the hardscape and the softscape. They tastefully soften architectural lines of buildings—expanses of wall, sharp corners, and rooflines. Exploit the

showing off stems

The twisted, ropy stems of mature, woody vines winding up posts of an arbor or pergola are ornamental in and of themselves. Prune new shoots along the lower parts of wisteria, honeysuckle, or kiwi vines to expose the bark at eye level. This also makes it easier to see and enjoy plantings in beds beneath the structure.

Hops features bristly stems that bear three- to five-lobed leaves. Female vines bear flowers that produce clusters of cone-like fruits used in beer-making. Hops vines are hardy to Zone 3.

English ivy, especially the large- or small-leafed, variegated varieties, covers vertical surfaces with masses of leathery, heart-shaped leaves year-round to Zone 5. Mature leaves are more rounded.

Mandevilla reveals tropical origins in its narrow leaves and funnel-shaped pink flowers. Twine it around lampposts and arbors for summer bloom. Hardy in Zone 10, but grown elsewhere as an annual.

Moonflowers wait until hot weather to produce 5-inch-wide, iridescent white flowers that last until frost. A night-blooming relative of morning glory, grown as an annual, its fragrant flowers attract moths.

versatility of those vines that also are willing to do groundcover duty, such as English ivy and wintercreeper, to create a seamless transition between horizontal and vertical planes on your property. The changing color of the leaves of many deciduous vines, such as Boston ivy and Virginia creeper, creates a colorful, living mural. Vines also help set a tone. Who doesn't immediately sense the mood of a home described as a vine-covered cottage? To reinforce an informal look, allow your

Tropical kiwi thrives in zones 8 to 10 of the South and West and produces the familiar fuzzy fruits found in grocery stores around the country. Use both female and male plants to produce fruits.

Kolomitka vine is actually a hardy kiwi with wonderful ornamental foliage. Mature leaves, marked with blotches of pink and white, turn an ordinary wall into a mural of color. It's hardy to Zone 4.

Morning glory evokes memories of old-time gardens. Its funnel-shaped flowers—from white to reds and blues—casually scramble over fence posts and walls. It's a fast-growing annual.

Passion flower looks as exotic as it sounds. Its 4-inch flowers are blue to white, with intricate centers. It's cold-hardy only to Zone 7 but is often grown as an annual in the northern states.

choosing a vine (cont'd.)

vines to roam at will by using permissive pruning. Annual vines and rambling types of roses (not vines, but very long-stemmed shrubs), both of which tend to be quite rambunctious, are great choices for an informal look. To add formality, choose more substantial, decorous perennial vines. Prune them strictly to maintain a dignified shape. ❧Vines are an important element in a backyard wildlife habitat.

They shelter birds, which like to have cover where they can perch in view of the bird feeder and check for predators before visiting it. Also, the stiff stems of woody perennial vines provide solid support for nests. Many vines, such as kiwis and grapes, bear

using vines as camouflage

Temporarily cover landscape eyesores with annual vines. Because they grow so rapidly, they effectively mask rotting stumps, new utility boxes, compost piles, and construction fencing. Let them climb dying trees and shrubs that you'd rather not remove right away. When the vines die back in fall, the weather will be cool enough to deal with those problems.

❧**Purple passion flower,** called purple granadilla, bears 3-inch-long, purple edible fruit. This variety, hardy in Zone 10 only, has three-lobed leaves, each 4 to 6 inches long with wavy edges.

❧**Sweet autumn clematis** billows over walls, pergolas, and arbors all summer long. In mid-August it produces clouds of small, fragrant, white flowers. This vine is cold-hardy to Zone 5.

❧**Wintercreeper** has evergreen leaves, either green or variegated with cream or yellow. Its thin, shrubby stems creep overland or climb a variety of vertical surfaces. It's hardy as far north as Zone 5.

❧**Wisteria** takes time out from twining around any handy—but strong—support to bear cascades of fragrant, lavender or white, pea-shaped flowers in May. It's cold-hardy to Zone 5.

fruit and are a rich source of food. Many flowers, such as climbing hydrangea, moonflower, and sweet autumn clematis, attract beneficial insects, bees, and butterflies. And hummingbirds enjoy the nectar from honeysuckle, trumpet vine, and mandevilla.

Virginia creeper, hardy to Zone 3, decorates walls with leaves divided into five leaflets, each 2 to 5 inches long. In the fall, they turn scarlet, setting off the blue berries that appear at the same time.

Yellow (golden) clematis has two things going for it—beautiful, 3- to 4-inch-wide flowers that bloom in late summer and attractive seedheads that develop after its blooms fade. It's hardy to Zone 5.

growing grapes

Grapevines are ornamental as well as edible. Display them attractively in a formal espalier design that looks elegant, yet provides desirable light and air to promote fruiting.

Encourage grapevines to cover a decorative arbor. It provides a sturdy base and is open to lots of light and air above and below it. The grapes are easy to harvest at the peak of ripeness.

Train grapes to grow on a chain link enclosure to obscure the fence's utilitarian appearance. Its crisscross design provides lots of places for the grapevines to attach securely.

Grapevines cling easily to a stair railing or other architectural feature. When you prune them to promote maximum fruiting, you simultaneously control their growth.

A pergola gives grapevines plenty of area to expand. The fruit dangles attractively between the many horizontal supports—and is within reach when you're ready to pick it.

supporting vines

The constantly growing stems of vining plants need something to hold onto, or they will sprawl on the ground. You need to provide an appropriate support system for them. The strength of your structure will vary by type of vine. Some require extremely sturdy materials that will hold them up for many years. Wisteria, grape, and kiwi, which live for decades, grow increasingly bulky and heavy over time. Others, like annual vines, are relative lightweights. Because they live only for a season and die when frost arrives, their stems are relatively slim, and their mass—mostly leaves—doesn't strain most supports. The design of the support is a key factor, too, because vines attach

weather

Free-standing tepees and structures such as arbors and pergolas are vulnerable to harsh winds and rain, especially if they're supporting mature vines. Make sure the structure you're using is sturdy enough to support the combined weight of heavy, wet leaves and flowers or fruits against the strong winds and heavy rains of summer storms.

Tepees (or the more-formal tuteurs) support vines in vegetable and ornamental gardens. Tie string between the poles to help nasturtiums, scarlet runner beans, morning glory, and others twine as they climb.

You can buy special vine clamps that wedge into a masonry wall and support vines that can't hold on by themselves. Push the clamps into the mortar, then guide and fasten vine stems to them.

English ivy develops tiny aerial roots along its stems, called holdfasts that enable it to grip surfaces without support, but that penetrate cracks and holes.

The stems of some vines, such as garden peas, produce dainty yet strong tendrils that curl around a narrow support and allow them to climb upward.

themselves in a variety of ways. Choose a support to accommodate each vine's growing style and future size. Some vines are *clingers*. English ivy, for example, forms sticky, hairy rootlets, called holdfasts, along its stems that attach directly to the surface on which it's growing. Clingers don't need special support and get along quite well on walls and other handy surfaces such as tree trunks. However, their rootlets can damage old or loose mortar in brick or stone walls, so check the mortar carefully before you plant clingers. Lots of vines— wisteria, morning glory, honeysuckle, and kiwi,

strangler warning

Never use a living tree as a support for a woody perennial twining vine. The vine will wrap around the trunk or branches and then, as the tree and vine stems grow wider, the vine girdles the tree, strangling it. Over the years, the pressure of the vine cuts off the tree's circulation, and it dies. Wisteria is a common offender.

59

It's easy to train twiners (vines that encircle supports with their main stems) to climb a support. This morning glory, after some gentle encouragement, will attach to the fence and cover it rapidly.

A trellis makes a lot of sense for young vines with flexible stems. Thread the tips of vines, such as this clematis, through the spaces and around the crosspieces while they still bend easily.

A support for a twiner, such as morning glory, needs vertical members. If it doesn't, string lengths of twine or wire vertically to create twining paths for it.

contrasting colors

Before you paint a support, consider the color of the leaves and flowers of the vine. Go for contrast. Here, you don't get the full impact of the lovely white wisteria blooms against a white trellis, but you do appreciate them against the green wall.

supporting vines (cont'd.)

among others—are *twiners*. They climb by winding their stems around supports. Because they can't fasten themselves to anything as they're attempting to curl their way up a vertical element, wrap a wire or string around the new, young plants to help them get started. Then when they reach a horizontal member, they can hitch onto it and be on their way. Still other vines are *grabbers*. They develop special tendrils—sort of modified leaf stems—that grasp a nearby support as they ascend. Grabbers such as passion flower, cross vine, and sweet pea have tendrils that are thin and tender, so they do best on narrow materials such as wire,

combining vines

Create a special effect by combining annual and perennial vines on the same support. Or, pair one that produces gorgeous flowers with one that has exceptional leaves. For example, encourage a free-flowering vine, such as morning glory, to weave among and through the stems of one with special leaves, such as Kolomitka vine. Or let clematis clamber around a fence laden with Dutchman's pipe. Grow morning glory and moonflower together for flowers day and night.

Pergolas are ideal for heavy-duty vines, such as grape, wisteria, and trumpet creeper. The many large, open spaces offer good light and air circulation. Be sure to sink the posts in concrete.

This giant bean tepee is substantial enough to support a ladder and several vines laden with beans. When the vines mature and the beans are ready for harvest, the ladder comes in mighty handy.

Lattice is an extremely versatile and useful vine support. You can fashion it into a free-standing structure or mount it on a wall as a trellis. And it provides attractive screening after annual vines die.

Give your gazebo summertime privacy—and a beautiful, though temporary, facade—by enclosing it with latticed walls covered with flowering vines, such as this thriving honeysuckle.

chain link fencing, netting, or narrow trellis bars. ¶Some plants called vines aren't vines at all. Climbing roses don't climb by themselves—they are shrubs with very long stems (canes) that you can coax to grow upward. Because they have no attachment mechanisms, they're basically *leaners,* and their canes lie against any vertical support that's handy. You can train them by loosely tying the canes to a structure, such as an arbor or pillar, that can bear their weight and guide them vertically.

A hand-hewn trellis like this one is especially appropriate for an informal setting. The honeysuckle effectively joins forces with its rustic support to contribute old-fashioned beauty to the scene.

Regardless of the design you choose, never fasten a support structure tightly to a wall. Leave about 6 inches between wall and trellis to permit air circulation and simplify the pruning process.

Accommodate small vines by adding lightweight trellises made of vinyl, bamboo, or wood lath to your walls. Clematis, cardinal flower, morning glory, or sweet peas create a lacy pattern like this one.

A matrix of wire fastened to the garage wall supports a honeysuckle, Kolomitka vine, and a nearby clematis. Thread heavy wire back and forth between screw eyes to make the support network.

planting and training vines

Plant vines and other climbers as you would any plant. Choose a location to fit its requirements for light and moisture. Perennial vines, such as wisteria and kiwi, are likely to be in place for many years, so select a site accordingly. Remember that flowering and fruiting vines need at least six hours of sun daily. Whether the roots of the plants you buy are bare, in container soil, or wrapped in burlap, be sure to keep them moist while you prepare the soil. ❧Newly planted vines start slowly. Annuals wait for warm weather for their big growth spurt. Perennials, which will be around for years, spend several weeks growing roots and leafing out and grow very little. Many take their

YOU WILL NEED

for planting:
- gloves
- trellis
- shovel or spade
- vine
- compost
- water

for training:
- gloves
- twine or other soft tie
- hand pruners

planting a vine

1 Place a trellis a few inches away from a wall to protect the wall and encourage air circulation. Set the trellis securely in the soil and brace it so it is stable enough to withstand the weight of a vine.

2 Dig the planting hole several inches in front of the trellis to allow room for the roots to spread and to avoid crowding the growing stems. Make the hole only as deep as its rootball.

3 Center the plant in the hole so the growing stems can fan out on both sides. Make sure the longest stems are against the trellis.

4 Add compost around the rootball, then fill in the hole with soil. Firm the soil over the roots, then water well.

entire first season to do so. Climbing hydrangea is notorious for its dawdling. The old saying, "The first year they sleep, the second year they creep, the third year they leap," aptly describes many perennial vines. ❦Nevertheless, you need to guide a vine's growth from the outset. Don't let stems flop on the ground. Instead, lead them to the base of their support, even if it means using a temporary stake until they can reach the bottom of the trellis. In some cases, you may need to prune them early to guide their growth. Cut off all but the sturdiest stems of twiners to start them winding around a post.

controlling vines

Vines need to be kept in their place. Clip and retie stems periodically on vines trained to trellises. Trim those clinging directly to brick or stone walls to prevent them from straying too far. Ivy tends to overwhelm windowsills and gutters and force its way under roof shingles. In midsummer, check its growth and prune back wandering stems.

training on a trellis

1 Train the longest branches to begin climbing the support. Tie each one—as shown with this barberry stem—loosely against the frame. The slack provides leeway for the branch to thicken.

2 Attach the stems with plastic twist ties (not ones with wire centers) that are easy to remove and adjust. Or use cloth strips, string, or nylon fishing line. Weave flexible stems directly through the mesh.

3 Trim extra stems at the base of the plant to direct energy to the longest stems. Trim fast-growing annual vines weekly once they get established.

4 Woody plants such as this barberry are slower growing and take years to climb a support. Early training pays off in future years with a lovely display.

63

regional groundcover and

	Spring	**Summer**
Cool Climates	❏ Sow seeds of annual vines indoors in early spring.	❏ Transplant annual vine seedlings into the yard in early summer.
	❏ As temperatures rise, remove winter mulch from beds.	❏ If rainfall is scarce, water grasses, vines, and groundcovers.
	❏ Prune perennial vines that bloom on new wood to stimulate flower and leaf buds.	❏ Edge groundcover beds to control any exuberant new growth.
	❏ Cut back ornamental grasses to make way for new shoots.	❏ Train new vines as they produce longer runners. Trim established ones.
	❏ Divide overlarge clumps of ornamental grasses into smaller chunks to plant elsewhere.	❏ Optional: Clip pieces of stem from groundcovers and vines to root in water or damp vermiculite.
	❏ Mow or burn (if legal) meadows and prairies.	
	❏ Fertilize perennial groundcovers and vines with a granular, slow-acting product.	
	❏ Renovate longtime groundcover plantings by cutting them back or mowing them at the highest mower setting. Topdress the area with organic matter to improve the soil.	
	❏ Plant new groundcovers, vines, and meadows.	
Warm Climates	❏ Sow seeds of annual vines indoors in early spring. Sow hardy ones directly outdoors.	❏ Transplant young homegrown or purchased annual vines outdoors.
	❏ Prune perennial vines that bloom on new wood to stimulate flower and leaf buds.	❏ If rainfall is scarce, water grasses, groundcovers, and vines.
	❏ Cut back dried fronds of ornamental grasses and divide them into smaller plants, if necessary.	❏ Trim groundcovers that overgrow their boundaries.
	❏ Plant new groundcover beds or extend and renovate established ones.	❏ Train vines as their growth spurts by tying main stems and pruning stray branches.
	❏ Rake, weed, and trim vine and groundcover plantings as growth proceeds.	❏ Optional: Clip pieces of stem from groundcovers and vines to root in water or damp vermiculite.

vine care checklist

Fall

- ❑ Continue to water groundcovers and vines in dry periods.
- ❑ Continue to edge and clip groundcover beds and climbing vines.
- ❑ As weather chills, move vines growing in containers to a sheltered area.
- ❑ After hard frost, mulch in-ground vines and beds of non-evergreen groundcovers.

Winter

- ❑ Record information on the selections, care, and performance of vines and groundcover plantings—especially new ones—over the past season.
- ❑ Drain gasoline and oil from power equipment and check spark plugs.
- ❑ Clean and sharpen garden tools to guard against rust.
- ❑ Order seeds and seedlings from mail-order nurseries and suppliers.

- ❑ Plant vines and groundcovers when weather cools.
- ❑ Plant or overseed meadows and prairies.
- ❑ Divide overlarge clumps of groundcover plants into several smaller plants to locate elsewhere or give away.
- ❑ Shape up planted areas by trimming plants, clearing debris, and spreading fresh mulch.
- ❑ Continue to train vines by tying them to supports. Trim only if necessary, because it will stimulate new growth that may not survive winter chill.

- ❑ In warmest zones, continue to plant and tend groundcovers. Weed and mulch as necessary.
- ❑ Record information on the selections, care, and performance of vines and groundcover plantings—especially new ones—over the past season.
- ❑ Drain gasoline and oil from power equipment and check spark plugs.
- ❑ Clean and sharpen garden tools to guard against rust.
- ❑ Order seeds and seedlings from mail-order nurseries and suppliers.
- ❑ Prune grapes toward the end of winter before their sap begins to rise.

trees and shrubs

the value of trees

Trees are the unsung heroes of our landscapes. Individually and collectively, in yards across the nation, they contribute enormously to our quality of life—even though they are largely taken for granted. However, when a tree is cut down or falls in a storm, the hole it leaves in the sky reminds us of its extreme importance. The wonderful hardwood forest that greeted the European settlers on the east coast of North America helped sustain them, just as it had the native population eons before. It sheltered abundant wildlife to hunt, yielded fruits and nuts to eat, and preserved the soil for agriculture. Its wood warmed and housed the settlers. It moderated the heat, blocked the wind, and caught the rain. So as the settlers migrated westward in their restless search for more and better land and opportunities, they carried in their being the sense that trees are part of a good life. Even the farmers among them—although they cleared trees to make fields for crops—knew how essential it was to preserve some of the trees. For settlers, trees were an integral part of the home

columnar

Columnar trees are shaped like columns or cylinders, with branches of uniform length—top to bottom. They aren't necessarily narrow, but they appear to be because of the branching pattern. Many commonly known trees are available in columnar versions.

examples:
Cherry, crabapple, European hornbeam, Lombardy poplar, red maple, quaking aspen, sugar maple, tuliptree

open-head irregular

The branching pattern of these trees is irregular and random, creating an open, asymmetrical canopy shape. They offer wonderful shade, and after their leaves fall, their branch architecture creates dramatic silhouettes against a winter sky.

examples:
Ash, buckeye, catalpa, hickory, pawpaw, sycamore (London plane), silver maple, smoketree

weeping

The branches of weeping trees droop downward and are covered with graceful cascading foliage. These typically smaller, ornamental trees soften the hardscape. Many commonly known trees are available in a weeping form.

examples:
Birch, cherry, crabapple, hemlock, katsura, larch, sourwood, willow

pyramidal

These broad, cone-shaped trees have triangular canopies—wider at the base and narrower toward the top. Many deciduous trees and conifers have this classic shape. The large ones are stunning on properties where they have room to grow.

examples:
American beech, American holly, baldcypress, blue spruce, cucumber magnolia, fir, linden, oak (pin, scarlet), sweetgum

landscape, wherever their home would be. Understandably, one of the great trials of life on the prairie was the absence of trees—living entities that seemed to sustain the human spirit as well as guard the environment and beautify the landscape. ❧Today, trees still nurture us. They provide continuity with our history and influence our climate and quality of life. We plant trees to make our properties more beautiful, valuable, and comfortable. They define our yards by establishing their scale, marking their borders, and roofing them with leafy canopies. By filtering light and creating shade, trees make our homes more livable. They contribute shelter and food to wildlife, health to the overall landscape, and beauty to all of us in the form of lovely flowers, fruit, and bark. And they enhance our properties' values, as well. Each healthy, mature shade tree can contribute up to $1,500 toward the value of a lot.

globe

The canopies of these trees—with their regular, rounded shape—are ideal for formal landscapes. Stately rows provide a strong linear feature, softened by the billow of their canopies. When alone on a spacious lawn, they make handsome specimens.

examples:
American hornbeam, American yellowwood, bur oak, black maple, flowering dogwood, hackberry, redbud

fastigiate

These trees have an elongated, narrow, tapering profile and a strong vertical habit that draws the eye upward. When planted in rows, they serve beautifully as hedges to define boundaries, as windbreaks, and as effective screens against noise or undesirable views.

examples:
Arborvitae, baldcypress, European beech, ginkgo.

vase

Trees that have vase-shaped canopies work well near streets and walks because they don't block the view of traffic or pedestrians. Branches grow at a sharp upward angle from the trunk, flaring outward at the tips. Canopies resemble upside-down triangles.

examples:
Boxelder, elm, fringetree, hawthorn, striped maple, zelkova

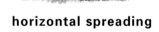

horizontal spreading

With strongly horizontal branches, even at the top of the canopy, these trees seem very wide. Usually massive, they overwhelm small properties and can dwarf single-story homes. But their spreading habit contrasts well with a narrow house.

examples:
Beech, Eastern redcedar, fir, honeylocust, hornbeam, Korean dogwood, larch, oak (red, white), witchhazel

choosing trees

Because trees can live for decades—even centuries in some cases—it's important to choose varieties that are appropriate for their site. Take time to consider what you want the tree to do—just look pretty, shade the driveway, block the wind or neighbor's view, or provide flowers or fruit. Will it be part of a formal planting area or grove, or will it stand alone? Consider its size at maturity. Will there be enough room for it? A tree's growth rate also may have a bearing on your choice. The slower-growers are hardwoods and tend to live longer. If it's important to establish shade or have flowers relatively quickly, choose a fast-growing tree. Typically, they're smaller, have soft

judging tree size

A small tree is not always a young tree. If it's small from lack of vigor, the condition of its bark will give it away. A weak one will have thicker bark that's textured with ridges, furrows, or flakes, rather than the smooth, tender bark of youth.

Japanese maples grow 3 to 20 feet tall and offer fine-textured foliage, rich color, interesting shapes, and a tolerance for some shade. Use them to adorn beds, pools, and lawns. Hardy in zones 3 to 6.

Callery pear is fast-growing and has small, white flowers in the spring and colorful foliage in the fall. Its pyramidal canopy reaches 30 to 45 feet at maturity. Early versions called Bradford tend to split in storms, so choose 'Aristocrat' or 'Chanticleer'. Hardy to Zone 4.

Korean dogwood has white spring flowers with pointed petals. Dangling, fleshy red fruits hang from its distinctly horizontal branches in fall. Zones 6–9.

Citrus trees bear lovely, fragrant, white flowers and edible fruits. These small trees easily deteriorate if you don't spray them properly. Zones 9 and 10.

wood, and don't live as long. ❧Scale trees to their surroundings. Use small or medium-sized varieties for smaller houses and yards. On any site, put smaller trees near the house and taller ones farther out in the yard or at its edge. ❧Trees and shrubs are either deciduous or evergreen. *Deciduous* trees lose their leaves in the fall and are bare all winter, though the leaves often give a final show of beautiful colors before they drop. *Evergreen* trees and shrubs retain their foliage year-round. Some, such as southern magnolia, feature broad leaves. Others, such as pines, have needled foliage.

Crabapple grows 15 to 25 feet tall and is covered in spring with deep pink flower buds that become white blossoms; they, in turn, give way to small red or yellow apples that the birds love. The tree spreads to an irregular shape. Zones 3–5.

Honeylocust is tough and adaptable, grows 30 to 50 feet tall, and drops pods. Its foliage turns yellow in fall. Choose the thornless variety. Zones 3–9.

Redbud bears tiny pinkish purple flowers along its stems and bare branches in early spring. They give way to rows of wide heart-shaped leaves. Pods become visible as leaves turn yellow in fall. Mature trees grow 25 to 30 feet tall. Zones 5–9.

Saucer magnolia is deciduous and grows to about 30 feet tall. It bears 6-inch-long, pale pink flowers early in spring. Hardy to Zone 6.

choosing trees (cont'd.)

Of course, there are always exceptions. The soft, fine-textured needles of larch and baldcypress turn color in the fall and then drop off—just to confuse things. ❧Every kind of cultivated tree has assets that suit it for some landscape use. Each also has certain requirements that are critical to its survival in the yard. Some are more cold-hardy than others, so check their hardiness-zone rating.

Many do best in rich, moist, woodsy soil that's definitely on the acid side. Others prefer more alkaline soil that tends to be dry because it's not as rich in moisture-holding organic matter. Some trees, like swamp red maples and baldcypress, can handle

urban trees

Certain trees are more tolerant of typical urban conditions than others. They're able to handle atmospheric pollutants from industry and cars, compacted soil, poor drainage, night lighting, and salt spray from snow plows. Typically, city trees have much shorter lifespans than their suburban or country counterparts. Those that do best are: Norway maple, oaks, Washington hawthorn, ginkgo, honeylocust, sweetgum, crabapple, linden, and zelkova.

Serviceberry is a tough and adaptable large shrub or small tree at 6 to 20 feet tall. Its early spring clouds of white flowers become edible dark fruits by June. Yellowish pink fall foliage entertains in a woodland setting or near a patio. Hardy to Zone 4.

White cedar is a type of falsecypress that grows to a narrow, conical 40 to 50 feet tall. It begins with a slender shape, then turns spirelike when it matures. At home in the eastern part of the U.S., it has light green or grayish foliage and likes wet soil. Zones 4–8.

Sorrel, or sourwood, grows to 75 feet tall and is a multiseason beauty. Its July flowers are drooping strands of tiny white urns among slightly leathery and glossy, medium green leaves that turn to a brilliant red early in the fall. Hardy to Zone 5.

Willow oak has narrow and pointed foliage and forms a fine-textured, dense conical canopy rising to about 50 feet at maturity. It makes a good street and shade tree and is easy to transplant. Foliage turns yellow before it drops in the fall. Hardy to Zone 6.

even truly wet soil. ¶Trees also have their liabilities. Some have thorns that make them unsuitable for homes with children. Others are weedy; some are messy—sycamores and the relatives of the London plane tree drip fuzzy balls, bark, and twigs all over the place. The spiked balls from sweetgum trees and the runaway roots of willows present challenges as well. However, if you choose the right place for some of these less-desirable varieties, you often can overlook their faults and enjoy their virtues instead.

Tuliptree grows quickly to its 25-foot height. Beautiful tulip flowers with orange centers snuggle among interesting leaves. Hardy to Zone 5.

Weeping cherry varieties typically grow 15 to 25 feet tall and spread as wide. They bear a blizzard of pink or white, single or double flowers. Zones 6–9.

Pine foliage is evergreen for year-round beauty and is comprised of bundles of soft, long needles. Though some pines are a bit brittle in harsh weather, they're often used for wind and privacy screening. Hardy in various zones, depending on variety of tree.

Spruce trees are fragrant needled evergreens —perhaps the ultimate Christmas tree. They range in height from dwarves no more than 5 feet tall to giants that tower over 100 feet high. Depending on variety, the hardiness range extends as cold as Zone 3.

choosing shrubs

A yard without shrubs is, well, not really a yard. With all their wonderful diversity of size, shape, foliage, and flower, shrubs can turn a mundane piece of property into a beautiful showplace. Shrubs make the yard inviting and livable. You've probably noticed that builders always plant a few shrubs around newly constructed homes. There may be no trees or grass, but there are shrubs.

Shrubs, with their deciduous or evergreen foliage, are enormously decorative and highly useful. Like trees, evergreen shrubs may have broadleaf or needled foliage and can offer colorful berries or cones, interesting bark, and lovely flowers. Even in the winter, their leafless, contorted trunks and

weather

In many areas of the country, rainfall is never generous. And it's becoming less dependable in many other areas, too. If you live where water is likely to be restricted, choose shrubs that don't require much water. Some examples are olive, butterfly bush, potentilla, and barberry.

American holly can grow 30 to 40 feet tall and is pyramidally shaped. This hardy evergreen has leathery, glossy, spined leaves. Female trees bear red or yellow berries that attract birds. Hardy to Zone 5.

Andromeda, or pieris, is a 4- to 12-foot tall, broadleaf evergreen. It bears pendulous clusters of fragrant, white, urn-shaped florets in the spring. This slow-growing shrub likes some shade. Zones 6–9.

Forsythia bears rows of bright yellow, trumpet-shaped flowers on its bare stems in early spring. It becomes 8 to 10 feet tall. Hardy to Zone 5.

Harry Lauder's walking stick is actually a filbert used as an ornamental shrub. It has coarse, veined leaves and grows 8 to 10 feet tall. Zones 4–9.

interesting architecture enhance the landscape. Their size provides a pleasant transition between tall trees and groundcover plantings, softening the edges of boundaries, foundations, buildings, and walls. At the same time, they protect the soil and support and shelter all kinds of wildlife. Shrubs are versatile. Use them as groundcovers on slopes, as living walls, as backdrops for flower borders, and as screens to block street noise and dust. Put them where they'll obscure landscape eyesores, such as heating and cooling units, swimming pool mechanicals, utility meters, and trash can areas.

avoiding deer damage

Visiting deer damage shrubs by nibbling their twigs, fruit, and foliage. Homeowners across the country are searching for ornamental shrubs that deer will ignore. Lists vary by region— even by neighborhood— but certain types of plants appear on many of them. Consider shrubs with thorns or prickers, resinous wood, aromatic foliage, and silver or gray fuzzy leaves.

Boxwood is an evergreen covered with tiny, oval, glossy leaves. It tolerates shearing into hedges very well. Common boxwood grows to 20 feet tall and accepts sun or light shade. Hardy to Zone 6.

Sumac grows up to 20 feet tall and bears clusters of greenish yellow flowers in late summer. Its foliage puts on a show of flaming red, yellow, or orange in the fall. It can form colonies in poor soil. Zones 4–9.

Japanese barberry grows 2 and 5 feet tall and is tough and versatile, even in poor, dry soil. Its small red berries persist all fall. Hardy to Zone 5.

Korean stewartia has delicate white blossoms in early summer. Its leaves turn orange-red in the fall, then drop to expose patchy bark. Zones 5–7.

choosing shrubs (cont'd.)

Use shrubs to accent pools, patios, and dooryards. Or plant thorny varieties to redirect children and animals using your yard for shortcuts. ❧Conifers are generating renewed interest. These cone-bearing, needled evergreens are available in dwarf forms—a much more suitable scale for today's smaller properties. They offer an amazing array of foliage color—soft blue, variegations in yellow or cream with green, as well as the traditional green. Whatever the colors, they really stand out in a winter landscape. Conifers also come in many forms—weeping, prostrate, and topiary, in addition to the usual upright configuration. ❧Native shrubs

using native shrubs

Native shrubs that combine the virtues of beauty and low maintenance include:

- *American arborvitae*
- *American beautyberry*
- *American holly*
- *Bayberry*
- *Bottlebrush buckeye*
- *California lilac*
- *Carolina allspice*
- *Chokeberry*
- *Dwarf fothergilla*
- *Mountain laurel*
- *Oakleaf hydrangea*
- *Oregon grapeholly*
- *Rhododendron (some)*
- *Serviceberry*
- *Sweet pepperbush*
- *Viburnum (some)*
- *Virginia sweetspire*

Lace-cap hydrangea features flat clusters of tiny, tight, fertile flowers ringed by petaled, sterile ones. The blue or pink flowers nestle among green foliage in early summer. Hardy to Zone 6.

Pyracantha (firethorn) branches are covered with thorns. They bear white flowers in spring that become bright orange or red berries by fall. Its smallish, oval leaves are evergreen. This shrub is easy to grow but difficult to prune. Zones 5–9.

Lilac boasts fragrant sprays of tiny, tubular florets in pink, white, and shades of lavender during the spring. Heart-shaped, smooth, bluish green leaves continue through the season and drop in the fall. Lilac grows slowly but lives a long time. Zones 4–9.

Plum-leaf azalea, native to the Southeast, bears its fragrant, orange-red flowers in midsummer, later than most azaleas. Shrubs have evergreen foliage and grow to 10 feet or more. Zones 5–8.

also are enjoying long-overdue attention. Because they have existed in the same region since long before European settlers arrived, they're very adapted to local climate and soil conditions. Unfortunately, Americans temporarily lost interest in them, while other countries happily adopted them. But now we're recognizing their many low-maintenance virtues. They don't require extra watering and tend to resist pest insects and disease. And they're big favorites of local wildlife.

attracting wildlife

Some shrubs with berries that attract birds and other wildlife include:

- *Barberry*
- *Bearberry*
- *Beautyberry*
- *Blueberry*
- *Brambles*
- *Cotoneaster*
- *Dogwood*
- *Euonymus*
- *Firethorn*
- *Holly*
- *Juniper*
- *Viburnum*
- *Wax myrtle*

Mountain laurel is a broadleaf evergreen that grows to 15 feet tall. It's vigorous and bears globes of intricate, starlike florets in late spring. Use it as a specimen or in woodland settings. Zones 4–9.

Oleander tolerates heat, drought, and salt and takes any soil. Narrow evergreen foliage lines thin branches tipped with colorful flowers all season. Caution: All parts of the plant are poisonous. Zone 9.

PJM rhododendron is a compact evergreen that grows 3 to 6 feet tall. Resembling an azalea, its leaves are small and leathery, turning purplish in the fall. Spring flowers are pinkish-lavender. Zones 4–9.

Seven-sons flowers soft green foliage shows off its 6-inch-long clusters of fragrant ivory flowers in late summer. It likes moist, woodsy soil (but tolerates less) and grows to 15 feet. Zones 5–8.

four-season interest

of a shrub. Even if your main priority is to use shrubs for a practical purpose, such as to prevent soil erosion or screen the view of the neighbors, hold out for types that can bring beauty to your yard during one or more seasons. Every shrub will have its particular showy feature at some point, so the trick is to choose an assortment of shrubs that have a variety of peak times. That way, you'll have something attractive to enjoy all year long. A peak time isn't necessarily limited to showy blossoms—it also might include incredible fall foliage color and dramatic pods, nuts, bark texture, or overall form. Another way to achieve year-

spring

Scotch broom grows quickly to 6 feet. Lined with fragrant, yellow, pealike flowers in midspring, its bare, bright green stems add color to the yard in winter. Zones 6–9.

Flowering dogwood offers white or pink spring flowers and scarlet fall foliage and berries that are favorites of birds. It can grow to 40 feet in an irregular pattern. Zones 5–8.

Crapemyrtle bears clusters of crinkly petaled flowers in shades of pink and white in summer at tips of branches. Its flaking, patchy bark and sinuous shape give winter interest. Zones 6–9.

California lilac grows 4 to 6 feet tall with white or pink spring flowers and bears showy, bright red seed capsules in summer. Its leaves turn yellowy tan in fall. It likes dry soil. Zones 4–6.

Korean azalea (*foreground above*) is a deciduous rhododendron with magenta flowers that appear on leafless stems in early spring. It is lovely paired with magnolia or forsythia. Zones 4–8.

Doublefile viburnum has a double row of white flowers along its branches in spring that give way in summer to bright red berries that attract birds. It grows 6 to 12 feet tall. Zones 3–8.

round beauty is to choose those special shrubs that are constantly interesting, such as evergreen hollies. Their shiny leaves are attractive year-round and the berries in fall through winter—only on female shrubs—are an added bonus. ❧Choose specimens that will give a succession of bloom. You'll find many that bloom over the summer into fall—even winter in the coldest states. Add witchhazel (late-winter bloomer), serviceberry (early-spring bloomer), and crapemyrtle (summer bloomer) to your mix. Follow up with fall-blooming Japanese bush clover or sweet autumn clematis if they're suitable for your region.

summer

Bluebeard, or blue spirea, blooms in late summer. The scented blue flowers blend nicely with its gray-green foliage. The leaves and stems are scented, too. It takes dry, sunny sites. Zones 6–9.

Japanese rose, or kerria, grows 4 to 6 feet tall and creates yellow flowers in midspring on slightly arching branches. Its leaves yellow and drop in fall, revealing green stems for winter. Zones 4–9.

Colonnade™ apple is ornamental as well as productive. Spring blossoms yield colorful fruit by midsummer. Grows about 6 feet tall and 2 feet wide, perfect for a container. Zones 4–7.

Peegee hydrangea grows upright 6 to 12 feet tall and bears fat clusters of ivory blooms in midsummer. Flowers turn pinkish in fall, remain attractive all winter, and dry well. Zones 3–8.

Beach rose combines a sturdy constitution with lovely flowers. Textured, leathery leaves resist disease and look good all summer. Enjoy the orange hips through fall. Zones 2–7.

Rose daphne is a low-growing, fine-textured, mounded, semi-evergreen shrub—likely to keep its leaves in mild winters. It bears fragrant, bright pink flowers in spring. Zones 4–7.

four-season interest (cont'd.)

❧The word "ornamental" isn't just about flowering. It's also about berries and cones, bark texture and branching pattern, habit and silhouette. And mostly it's about leaves. The glory of many shrubs is their foliage. Sometimes it's the shape of the leaves, sometimes the color or variegation pattern, sometimes both. The appeal of needled evergreens, for example, is the fine texture and color of the needles on view all through the year—especially winter. Many deciduous shrubs, on the other hand, offer a bonus show of fall foliage color before the leaves drop. ❧Don't underestimate the value of colorful berries either. Hollies, firethorn, beautyberry, and others peak in the fall as their fruit ripens, then extend their ornamental duties well into winter. After frost, when the leaves have fallen,

fall

❧**Beautyberry** has inconspicuous flowers and plain green leaves. Suddenly, in late summer, clusters of vibrant magenta berries appear along the stems and remain through fall. Zones 5–8.

❧**Pyracantha,** or firethorn, follows up its white spring flower show with a fiery display of bright orange to red berries in fall. It's best in sun and dryish soil. Beware of thorns. Zones 6–9.

❧**Burning bush,** or winged euonymus, has distinctive flared stems covered by plain green leaves. In fall, its foliage turns a stunning crimson that lights up the yard before dropping. Zones 4–8.

❧**Wintergreen** is a low evergreen groundcover. Tiny white flowers become red berries that last from summer until spring and are fragrant when crushed. Leaves are reddish in winter. Zones 3–6.

❧**Aucuba** has dense, shiny evergreen leaves speckled with yellow, which upstage the purple spring flowers and red fall berries. In cold areas, take cuttings in fall and grow indoors. Zones 7–10.

❧**Japanese maples** are prized for their fall color—bright yellow, reddish orange, or deep scarlet. Some change leaf color from spring to summer as well. Many handsome varieties. Zones 5–9.

deciduous shrubs with textured and colorful bark can show it off—there are no more leaves to distract your sight. ❧Of course, the easiest way to assemble an assortment of shrubs that will provide beauty over the four seasons is to choose a few individual ones that have everything—or almost everything—going for them. Oakleaf hydrangea, for example, has gorgeous spring flowers that persist all summer, coloring gradually into ivory and pink as fall approaches. Its handsome green foliage takes on beautiful colors, eventually dropping to expose the shrub's rustic, peeling bark. Virginia sweetspire is another delight, offering spring flowers, decorative capsules, and colorful fall foliage.

winter

River birch, a handsome tree in any season, shows off in winter. In fall, its leaves turn yellow. Its bark—a patchy, reddish tan—peels back in strips to create gorgeous winter interest. Zones 3–9.

Paperbark maple has lovely bark that is overshadowed by leaves most of the year. Growing 20 to 30 feet tall, it boasts cinnamon brown, peeling bark that gets better as it ages. Zones 5–7.

Holly has handsome, spiny, glossy evergreen leaves, which dramatically set off the red or yellow berries that mature in midfall and last most of the winter. It attracts birds to the garden. Zones 5–9.

Japanese maples have sinuous branches and great architectural form that can be best appreciated after the leaves have dropped. A dusting of snow highlights the form. Hardy to Zone 5.

Witchhazel blooms from early to late winter, but there are fall- and spring-blooming varieties, too. Fragrant, yellow, ribbonlike flowers unfurl on sunny days. It boasts handsome fall color. Zones 5–8.

Cornelian cherry has dark green foliage that turns purplish in fall then drops to reveal flaky, gray-brown bark. In late winter, it bears flat, yellow flowers just before its leaves return. Zones 4–7.

attracting wildlife

Wildlife is an integral part of almost any backyard. Birds, butterflies, and other creatures add color, sound, and movement to the scene. At the same time, an assortment of wildlife is essential to a healthy landscape. Plants wouldn't survive without the help of pollinating and predator insects—or squirrels to bury nuts and seeds to grow new plants. Birds patrol for pest insects and eat those they find lurking in the bark of trees and shrubs and under the soil. In return, plants sustain the creatures by providing shelter in their dense branches and foliage and by supplying seeds, nectar, pollen, berries, bark, and cones for food. This reciprocal arrangement benefits all species in your yard.

weather

Seasonal storms are hard on backyard wildlife. Heavy winter snows, torrential spring rains, and summer/fall thunderstorms are stressful for birds, rabbits, squirrels, and others. Shrubs and trees, especially twiggy and heavy-foliaged ones, provide important shelter.

Gourd birdhouse trees appeal to purple martins. Site the gourds in an open area near fresh water to attract many insect-eating families.

Fresh water is essential to birds, insects, and butterflies, as well as to the occasional visiting duck or goose. Make sure it's available during the winter when natural sources freeze.

Pets help control undesirable wildlife. While cats occasionally may catch a bird, they also hunt voles, shrews, and mice. Dogs will chase deer.

trees and shrubs to attract wildlife

plant	part of the plant	wildlife it attracts
American beech	Nuts	squirrels, chipmunks, bears, porcupines
	Leaves	butterfly larvae
Buckeye	Flowers	hummingbirds
Butterfly bush	Flowers	butterflies, beneficial insects
Buttonbush	Flowers	bees, butterflies
	Seeds	ducks, deer
Cotoneaster	Berries	squirrels
Desert willow	Flowers	hummingbirds
Dogwood	Berries	squirrels, birds, rabbits
Glossy abelia	Flowers	hummingbirds
Hawthorn	Berries	birds
	Shelter	birds
Hickory	Nuts	squirrels
	Bark	insects for woodpeckers
Holly	Berries	birds
	Shelter	birds
Juniper	Cones	birds
Lilac	Flowers	bees, butterflies
	Leaves	deer
	Shelter	birds
Maple	Seeds	squirrels
Oak	Nuts	birds, squirrels, deer, wild turkey, raccoons, mice
Oregon grapeholly	Flowers	bees
	Berries	birds
	Shelter	birds, mammals
Paperbark birch	Seeds	birds
	Leaves	butterfly larvae
Pine	Cones	squirrels, chipmunks, birds
	Twigs	browsing game
	Shelter	squirrels, chipmunks, birds
Salal	Berries	chipmunks, birds, bears, deer
Serviceberry	Berries	songbirds, wild turkey, bear
Viburnum	Flowers	beneficial insects
	Berries	birds, chipmunks, fox, deer
	Shelter	birds, butterflies, larvae

attracting wildlife (cont'd.)

A yard that attracts and supports wildlife has lots of different kinds of plants. The more diverse the offerings of food and shelter, the more diverse the visitors. Include some native plants among them. Plant all kinds—trees and shrubs as the backbone—then vines, wildflowers, aquatic plants, and grasses. Choose annual and perennial flowers that are colorful, flat, and open faced. Herbs and many food crops also support wildlife. ¶But if you truly want to attract wildlife, don't use broad-spectrum pesticides, because they don't discriminate between good and bad pests and kill off the good guys, too. On top of this, the pest problems are likely to get

hedgerow habitat

Hedgerows are ideal for attracting wildlife. To start your own, choose from several types and sizes of shrubs—and perhaps vines—that offer a wide variety of berries, cones, and seeds over the entire year. The informal, somewhat unruly arrangement of these woody plants provides excellent cover for birds and small mammals, such as rabbits. They also require much less maintenance than a more formal hedge.

Viburnum varieties, such as highbush cranberry, black haw, and possum haw, produce spring flowers that have nectar for butterflies. In fall, their showy berries attract birds and deer. Zones 4–8.

Flowering dogwood bears fruits in late summer. Birds and squirrels wait and watch them redden before they descend and devour them. This doesn't affect the flowers the next spring. Zones 5–8.

Crabapple flowers attract honeybees and other insects in spring. By summer, they have developed into miniature apples that dangle enticingly from their branches. From late summer into fall—until the birds finish feasting—the red and gold hues of the fruit enliven the garden. Deer, rabbits, and foxes get the apples that drop to the ground. Zones 4–8.

worse, rather than better. Instead, use biological products on pest insects. And resort to barriers or repellents where certain animals, such as deer and rabbits, are unwelcome. ❧A yard that attracts wildlife offers housing. The best shelters for rabbits, chipmunks, hibernating butterflies, and birds that nest on or near the ground are brush piles and weedy grasses. Waterfowl prefer streams or ponds. Leaf litter and debris provide nesting materials. Hedges, shrubs, and trees supply cover and places to hang birdhouses.

Oregon grape holly is widely distributed across the country. A generous host to wildlife, its fragrant, yellow spring flowers are usually covered with honeybees. Its fall berries attract birds. Zones 6–9.

Butterfly bush is a magnet for adult butterflies. Its florets, packed in tapered clusters, are full of nectar. It begins to bloom in early summer when the butterflies appear. Zones 6–9.

Hibiscus flowers are classics for hummingbirds. They're trumpet shaped, the nectar deeply recessed for a perfect hummingbird fit. Red is the best color, then orange, yellow, pink, and purple. Zones 6–9.

Rose hips in shades of red and orange remain after garden roses have bloomed. People covet the vitamin-C-rich hips for jams and tea. Birds eat these brightly colored treats just as they are. Zones 2–7.

planting trees & shrubs

Trees and shrubs bought by mail order are often shipped with bare roots and arrive in late winter while they're still dormant. Deciduous ones have bare branches, their leaves having dropped the previous autumn. Evergreens do have their foliage, but they're also in their rest period. All the soil is washed off their roots, which are typically wrapped in moist, shredded paper, moss, or sawdust for shipment. This way, they're easy and relatively inexpensive to ship. Bare-root plants tend to be very young and therefore smaller than those sold in containers or balled and burlapped. They're less expensive, and many more varieties are available through specialty mail-order sources. ◤Keep plant

planting depth

Planting depth is critically important when you plant trees and shrubs. Regardless of whether they're bare root, containerized, or balled and burlapped, don't plant them too deeply. Check often while positioning them in the hole to assure that the root flare—the place where the roots begin at the base of the stems or trunk—is visible at or above the level of the ground.

YOU WILL NEED

- garden gloves
- shovel or spade
- bare-root plant
- bucket
- water
- mulch

planting bare-root trees and shrubs

1 Dig a hole that accommodates the roots when you spread them out. Make it deep enough so the soil mark—it's probably still visible on the stem—ends up level with the soil surface.

2 Unwrap the roots carefully and gently rinse off any sawdust, moss, or debris so they're bare. Cleanly clip off any dead rootlets, and cut broken ones back to healthy tissue.

5 Cut away any broken or dead stems. Unless the shipping and planting instructions specifically tell you to cut away a portion of healthy top growth, don't prune anything more.

6 Set the crown of the plant— where the roots join the stem—over the soil cone and drape the roots evenly over its sides. Make sure the soil mark on the stem or trunk is at or above ground level.

roots moist if you'll be delaying planting. Keep them wrapped and stored in a cool, dark place. Several hours before planting, unwrap the roots and set the plant in a container of tepid water so that its roots are immersed. Be careful not to damage the roots. The tiny root hairs are important because they will spearhead the growth in the soil. Once planted and watered, bare-root plants need less water than others until they leaf out. Delay fertilizing until they produce stems and foliage growth.

heeling-in

Sometimes it's not possible to plant bare-root nursery stock promptly. Heeling it in—a sort of temporary planting— assures that the roots stay moist and protected during the delay. Dig a trench or slot in the soil or in a pile of leaves, mulch, or compost. Then set the tree or shrub so its roots lay in it. Cover the roots with soil or compost in a loose heap and wet it down thoroughly. You can keep plants heeled-in for up to 3 months.

3 Soak the roots in a bucket of tepid water for several hours so they can take up water. The more hydrated the plant's tissues are, the better it can handle the planting process.

4 Press loose soil at the bottom of the hole into a cone to support the root system. Make it high enough so the roots drape freely and the plant crown is level with the soil surface.

7 Fill the hole with the soil removed from digging. Pour water into the half-filled hole to help reduce air bubbles, settle the roots in position, and indicate if you need to adjust the depth.

8 Add the remainder of the fill soil up to ground level. Firm it gently over the root zone to support the plant. Press soil into a ridge to create a shallow reservoir to hold water.

9 Water again to settle the soil. Mulch with a 2- to 3-inch layer of chopped leaves or aged wood chips over the root zone. This will discourage weeds and keep the soil moist. Don't fertilize now.

planting trees & shrubs (cont'd.)

More and more trees and shrubs sold these days arrive in containers. In fact, some nurseries raise trees in them from the outset, and the first time they're ever in the ground and develop roots freely is when you plant them in your yard. Before you purchase a containerized tree or shrub, check to see if it's rootbound. Be suspicious if roots are swelling above the soil level, wrapped around the trunk, or trailing out the bottom of the container. Ask the salesperson to lift the plant out of its container so you can see if the roots are wrapped in circles around the soil ball. Choose a plant that's still comfortable in its pot. It will be less stressed and more willing to wait quite a while in case planting is delayed. The idea is to encourage the tree's or shrub's roots to leave

time to plant

Fall is the best time to plant many trees and shrubs. But spring is the next best time to plant and transplant and is preferable for certain trees, such as oaks, beeches, birches, and willows. You can plant those that come in containers almost any time the soil isn't frozen.

YOU WILL NEED

- garden gloves
- shovel or spade
- containerized plant
- burlap or tarp
- pruners
- water
- mulch material

planting container-grown trees and shrubs

1 Dig the planting hole just as deep as the tree's or shrub's container. Slope the sides a bit so the hole is wider near the top to encourage the roots to grow laterally outward into the soil.

2 Slide the root ball out of the container carefully. If the soil is moist, the ball should come out easily. If it's stubborn, check to see if roots protruding from the bottom of the pot are snagging it.

6 Fill the hole with the plain dirt that you dug from it. Don't add materials to improve it unless the ground is solid clay. The plant has to learn to handle its new soil environment.

7 Firm the soil around the buried root ball to remove any air pockets. Create a watering basin by mounding the soil several inches high just beyond the edge of the planting hole.

their pampered environment of loose, rich container soil and venture forth to find food and water on their own in a strange, more daunting soil. Don't put any special soil amendments in the hole or add them to the fill soil. They might encourage roots to stay put and wrap around themselves. Withhold fertilizer, which mainly fuels foliage growth, while the tree or shrub concentrates on root growth. Once the planting is established and new stems and foliage appear,

sprinkle some granular, slow-acting fertilizer over the root zone and let the rain soak it in. Use lots of organic mulch to keep the soil moist, and give the new tree or shrub plenty of moisture the first year or two. Water it in winter when the ground isn't frozen.

3 Loosen and untangle any circling or snarled roots. Cut any that are broken, dead, or hopelessly tangled. Those protruding from the soil ball will have a head start growing outward.

4 Loosen any bottom roots that have matted. If they don't free up easily, cut or slice through them to get them to hang freely. Cut off impenetrable masses. This won't harm the plant.

5 Set the plant in the empty hole. Step back to see if its orientation is pleasing. Then check its depth. The top of its soil ball should be even with, or slightly above, the surrounding ground.

8 Water the tree or shrub thoroughly, filling the reservoir, then letting it drain. Do this several times, waiting a while between waterings for the water to soak in deeply.

9 Stake trees only if they are threatened by wind. Insert two or three stakes into the soil, equidistant around the root zone. Loop soft tie material around the trunk and tie one loosely to each stake.

10 Mulch the root zone with a 2- to 3-inch layer of organic material, such as aged wood chips, pine needles, or chopped leaves. Don't pile mulch against plant stems, and don't fertilize at this

planting trees & shrubs (cont'd.)

❧Trees sold with their roots in soil wrapped in burlap tend to be larger and more mature. These B & B (balled and burlapped) trees grow in the ground and are dug in late winter or spring, wrapped, and shipped to garden centers. Sometimes the burlap-wrapped root ball is covered with a wire cage to stabilize it and make carrying easier. Although they're more difficult to handle, B & B plants generally transplant successfully. When properly cared for, they can sit safely for months at the nursery, where the root balls may be buried in mulch to keep them moist. When the tree is sold, its branches are bound loosely with twine to prevent damage during transport and planting. ❧In the past, suppliers traditionally used standard burlap because it's tough, its natural

getting off to a good start

Because the first priority for a newly planted tree or shrub is to establish and grow roots, use a kelp or mycorrhiza growth product at planting time to help it get started. Delay spreading granular, slow-acting fertilizer until the plant indicates its roots are established and functioning by showing new stem and leaf growth.

YOU WILL NEED

- shovel or spade
- burlap-wrapped plant
- tarp
- water
- mulch
- stakes (optional)
- tree wrap (optional)

planting balled and burlapped trees and shrubs

1 Examine the tree before you buy it. Reject those with gouges, scrapes, or wounds on the trunk. Look, too, for girdling roots encircling the base of the trunk under the burlap wrapping.

2 Spread a tarp for the soil. Dig a hole with sloping sides exactly as deep as the root ball is high and at least half again as it is wide. Don't add anything to the hole or soil.

5 Use the plain loose soil on the tarp to fill in the hole around the root ball. Water it when the hole is half full to prevent air pockets. Check the root ball level again and raise it if it has sunk.

6 Finish filling the hole and firm the soil. Form a ridge of soil just beyond the edge of the hole to create a water reservoir. Water slowly and deeply. Fill the reservoir and let it drain.

fibers rot in the hole, the soil around the roots isn't disturbed, and it makes planting easier. Today's "new" burlap is made from synthetic fibers. It's difficult to detect and doesn't decay in the soil. Cut away as much of it as possible from the sides of the root ball after you've positioned it properly in the hole. Because most roots grow laterally, this will ensure unobstructed progress. If the ball is encased in a wire cage, cut it away, too. Then you can get at the burlap and remove it.

staking a tree

1 Use straps around the tree's trunk if you have to stake it. The wide, soft material doesn't cause abrasions on its tender bark. Attach supporting wire or rope to the grommets in the straps.

2 Insert two or three stakes in the soil just outside the planting hole and equidistant around it. Attach a supporting wire or rope to each stake. Be sure to leave some slack in the wire or rope to allow the trunk to flex properly.

3 Never leave staking on a newly planted tree for more than six or eight months. Throughout this period, check the straps around the trunk to make sure they're loose enough to avoid damaging the tender bark.

3 Remove any protective outer wrapping, but leave the burlap on to hold the roots while you position the plant in the hole. Untie the branches to determine the most pleasing aspect.

4 Cut away as much burlap as you can. Roots grow laterally, so fabric under the ball can remain. Be sure the top of the root ball—where the roots flare out from the trunk—is at or above ground level.

7 Spread a 2- to 3-inch layer of organic mulch over the root zone to discourage weeds and retain soil moisture. Unwrap the branches if they remain tied. They will take time to regain their normal attitude.

8 Use tree wrap to protect the tender bark on young trees threatened by rodent and sun damage. Follow the instructions on the package to ensure proper application.

planting an evergreen

Because they're living walls, your hedges are prominent features of your landscape. So your choice of shrubs and the way you prune them can set a style for your entire yard. All kinds of shrubs have the qualities to make a good hedge. Tall or short, deciduous or evergreen, a shrub need only have a reasonably uniform growth habit, heavy branching, and attractive dense foliage. However, those intended for a formal hedge must be able to handle the close shearing they get on a regular basis. ¶The purpose of the hedge influences your choice of shrub. Faster-growing deciduous shrubs provide a better seasonal show— spring flowers, colorful fall foliage, and berries. They

instant hedge

One trick to hurry a hedge is to space the shrubs so they're actually too close together. This provides an instant hedge look. As the shrubs grow and start to crowd each other, dig up every other one and transplant them elsewhere. Alternatively, shrubs planted in a staggered pattern look like a filled-in hedge, even though they're the correct distance apart.

YOU WILL NEED

- shrubs
- stakes
- strings
- shovel or spade
- measuring tape
- water
- mulch

1 Choose nursery stock that's uniform in color, size, and shape. Check to see whether the roots are healthy and well-developed. Buy all the plants you will need at the same time and place.

2 Tie string to stakes to mark the area where the shrubs will be planted. The line will guide your digging so the bed will be straight and uniformly wide. Keep plants moist until planting.

5 Set the plants, still in their pots, along the trench to establish the correct spacing. Allow for their width at maturity, even though they may look very far apart at this stage.

6 Remove each plant from its container and check the roots. Loosen or untangle any that are matted from being confined in the pot. Clip off any broken ones.

hedge

also make good accents and boundaries. Evergreen shrubs—especially needled ones, such as juniper, arborvitae, or falsecypress—grow more slowly. Their year-round foliage provides privacy and shelter from wind. Shrubs with thorns—especially barberry, holly, and landscape roses—are particularly useful in a hedge that's a barrier to foot traffic and unwelcome visitors. ❦When you shop for needled evergreens, choose ones that have uniform size and color. Be sure all shrubs are healthy. If a sickly one dies after a couple of years, it can ruin forever the uniformity of the hedge. Choose a hedge site that has the appropriate amount of sun over its entire length, because any portion that's in the shade won't grow uniformly.

3 Dig within the string guides. Although it's possible to plant shrubs for a hedge in a row of individual holes, a trench is more efficient. Remove turf sod and put it aside, then dig the soil.

4 Dig the trench as deep as the containers in which the plants arrived. Slope the sides to encourage roots to grow outward. Don't put any loose material in the bottom of the trench.

7 Position the shrubs in the trench. Check that they are at the correct depth. Adjust them, if necessary, so that the tops of their root balls are at, or just above, ground level.

8 Fill in the trench with plain soil. Firm it gently over and around each root ball, then water well. Spread a 2- to 3-inch layer of organic mulch over the planted bed, then water again.

windbreaks

❦**Burlap** serves as a temporary windbreak for young evergreen shrubs in a site exposed to drying winter winds and sun. Remove it when spring arrives.

❦**Straw** stacked as bales forms a temporary wall to protect evergreens from wind and sun damage in the winter. Loose straw makes an excellent soil insulator.

planting a shrub border

Shrub borders are truly freewheeling affairs. Unlike hedges, where a considerable degree of uniformity of plant type, size, and design is necessary to achieve the correct look, shrub borders are all about diversity. Those that are the most attractive and interesting owe their beauty to their variety—in size and shape of plants, foliage color, and texture. Some also boast delightful seasonal displays of flowers, fruit, cones, or bark. The interplay of these features gives the borders structure and interest over all the seasons. ¶Although hedges are planted in more or less formal rows to achieve a linear effect, shrub borders may vary in width—and may even curve pleasingly. They will also vary in

YOU WILL NEED

- spade or shovel
- organic material
- garden rake
- shrubs (a mix of deciduous and evergreen)
- water
- pruners
- mulch

1 Site preparation is important if your planting area is new, or if your soil needs help. Remove sod and set it aside. Turn over the soil to loosen and aerate it.

2 Add organic material—compost, chopped leaves, or Canadian sphagnum peat moss—to improve soil's ability to hold water, drain, and add nutrients.

5 Start your layout by temporarily arranging the potted shrubs on the prepared soil. Then move them around until you find a pleasing composition.

6 Dig a hole for each plant exactly as deep as its container. For easy access, start at the back of the border and move to the front.

depth, depending on the site and purpose—15 to 20 feet deep to cover the area between a driveway and a wall, or only 6 to 8 feet deep. And they're typically longer than they are wide. Shrub borders work well on uneven ground, too. On a slope, they help control erosion while they do ornamental duty. When planted on a berm—a constructed mound of soil that raises the elevation along boundaries—a shrub border screens the noise and view of traffic. One that's composed of understory plants, such as azaleas, rhododendrons, and mountain laurel, makes a good transition between a woodland and the lawn area.

weather

Evergreen shrubs in a border often are exposed to harsh sun and wind during the winter. As a result, they're in danger of drying out, because their leaves continue to release moisture that their roots can't replenish if the ground is frozen. Shelter them with a windbreak and/or spray their foliage with an antidessicant before cold weather sets in.

95

3 Sprinkle granular, slow-acting fertilizer on the soil. Mix it in as you rake the soil smooth and level the bed. Remove any stones and debris.

4 Keep plants awaiting transplanting moist. Containers dry out rapidly, so set them in a sheltered area—in the shade if the weather is warm.

7 Prune discolored, broken branches while the shrubs are in their pots. You can spot problems easier when the plants are at eye level.

8 Set each shrub in its hole with the top of its root ball exactly at, or even slightly above, the adjoining surface. Fill in with extra soil, firm it gently, and water.

planting a shrub border (cont'd.)

A simple shrub border may be a bed of various ornamental shrubs planted more or less in a row. It may front a wall or fence, or even the foundation of the house or garage. A more elaborate one may accommodate several rows of shrubs of various heights. Plant them irregularly, staggered so that every one is on view from the front of the border. Position the taller ones toward the back, medium ones in the center, and low-growing and groundcover types at the front of the border. Leave plenty of space for them to grow to natural size at maturity—plus a bit more to allow you room to move between them to water, feed, and prune. You can plant a shrub border using only one type of shrub—for instance, just evergreens, or even just conifers. They're available in so many

optimizing space

Take advantage of the extra space at the front of your shrub border by planting some flowers. Incorporate a few hardy spring-blooming bulbs, such as daffodils, when you plant the bed. Add petunias or impatiens for the summer months, then replace them with chrysanthemums in the fall. Be careful not to disturb the shrubs' shallow root systems when you do your planting.

9 Some shrubs have unruly habits. Prune off excessively long or damaged branches. They are easier to handle while still in pots.

10 One by one, remove each plant from its pot. Loosen any roots that are tangled or wrapped around in circles. Or score the root ball with a knife.

13 Fill the hole with soil, firming it around the roots to eliminate air pockets. After watering, the soil may sink; add more soil if necessary to level the area.

14 Water the border after it's planted. To avoid compacting the soil, don't walk on it. The more aerated it remains, the more water it will hold.

colors, sizes, shapes, and textures that such a border can provide lots of year-round interest. Another option is to use a mixture of deciduous and evergreen shrubs. This gives you a perfect opportunity to incorporate shrubs that are popular with birds and other wildlife so you can develop a backyard wildlife habitat. Choose shrubs that are relatively self-reliant and need little maintenance. Allow them to develop their natural shape and size so you can minimize pruning. Choose shrubs that are well-suited to the soil as well as available light and water. Mulch them well to reduce weeds and keep soil moist.

11 Plant broadleaf evergreen shrubs the same way as needled evergreens. Dig a planting hole in prepared soil as deep as the container and a bit wider.

12 Adjust the depth so the shrub is at or above the level of the surrounding ground. Make sure each shrub has room to spread to its mature size.

15 Spread a 2- to 3-inch layer of organic material over the bare soil to discourage weeds, preserve moisture, and protect the soil.

16 For finishing touches, include colorful annuals near the front and edge of the border. In autumn, plant some hardy bulbs among the shrubs.

pruning woody plants

Pruning is essential to plant health and beauty. It disciplines growth and coaxes the best performance from woody plants, such as trees, shrubs, and perennial vines. Some homeowners who don't understand the process delay it too long or avoid it altogether, making their plants suffer. But pruning isn't all that difficult, if you know the specific need. ❧Prune *to repair* injury and prevent disease and insect problems whenever they arise, whatever the season. Jagged stubs from a broken branch provide an entry for disease and insects into the interior of the plant, so make a smooth cut near the base of the limb to promote healing. Prune out branches with tents that hold caterpillars. Eliminate

more pruning hints

- For your safety and for the health of your plants, keep your pruning equipment sharp. Don't leave pruners outdoors or they may rust and become dull.
- To prevent browning, clip the tips of needled evergreens when they're damp.
- Don't paint or seal wounds where tree limbs are removed. Exposure to air prevents decay while the healing callus tissue gradually grows over the area.
- Hire a professional if the job requires using a chainsaw on a ladder.

removing a large limb

1 Undercut the designated branch away from the trunk. This prevents a tear that may strip the bark down onto the trunk when you ultimately cut through the cumbersome, large limb from above.

2 Top-cut the limb just beyond the undercut. Make this cut all the way through the limb to remove it entirely. Because it's a preliminary cut, it doesn't have to be beautiful.

3 Remove the heavy limb before making a final, smooth cut. Identify the branch collar at the base of the branch. Cut the branch just beyond it.

4 This incorrect cut leaves a big stub instead of a small knob. The tissues in the branch collar cannot close such a large wound.

rubbing branches and weak crotches. ❧Prune *to train* the structure and stimulate growth of young plants while they're dormant in late winter. Thin crowded branches and saw off one of the competing branches to establish a single leader where necessary. Remove branches that rub on the roof. Shear hedges and renovate old, overgrown shrubs early in the season by cutting back all stems to the ground or removing just the thickest. ❧Prune *to reduce growth* or remove errant branches during the growing season. But don't expect to *control growth*, because many plants react to pruning by generating new leaves and flowers.

when to prune trees and shrubs

plant	when to prune	why
Andromeda	after spring bloom	shape growth; remove winterkill
Arborvitae	late winter when dormant	shape; prune out winterkill
Azalea	after spring bloom	shape growth
Barberry	spring/summer	shear for hedge; renovate/shape
Boxwood winterkill	late winter when dormant	shear as hedge; prune out
Butterfly bush	early spring	cut back stems to start new wood
Daphne	after flowering	shape growth
Falsecypress	late winter	shape
Forsythia	after spring bloom	shear for hedge; shape or renovate
Holly	winter, early spring	boughs for decoration; shape
Hybrid tea roses	late winter–early spring	remove winterkill, shape; stimulate new growth
Juniper	late winter	shear for hedge
Lilac	after spring bloom	groom: deadhead, remove suckers
Mock orange	after spring bloom	thin stems; trim unruly branches
Mountain laurel	after spring bloom	renovate overgrowth
Nandina	early spring	cut off dead berries; shape
Pine	late spring	clip "candle" growth for size
Rhododendron	after spring bloom	shape growth; deadhead flowers

pruning to reveal bark

You can improve a tree's appearance by removing its lower limbs, especially when it's young and just forming its branching structure. In its ungainly adolescence, it may develop branches that are too close together or that cross and rub bark against bark. Sometimes branches form at such a severe angle with the trunk that the crotches are weak and break easily in storms. In all of these cases, you'll want to prune excess or ill-formed limbs to improve the tree's health, as well as enhance its ornamental appeal. And if you selectively remove tree limbs, you can open up a tree's canopy to more light and air. ❧Limbing-up a tree—removing one or more lower limbs—is a common practice where trees

sprucing up

As Colorado blue spruces age, their lower limbs often become scraggly and flop on the ground. You can improve their appearance immensely by cutting off these unkempt branches to expose 6 to 8 feet of the trunk.

limbing-up a tree

1 Use loppers—long-handled pruners that require two hands—on branches up to 1 inch thick. Cut just beyond the branch collar to promote healing.

2 Remove low branches—those less than 6 feet above the ground—that block the way of pedestrians and lawnmower operators.

3 Proper cuts stimulate the branch collar, healing it to a rounded knob that's barely detectable on trunks covered with colorful, textured, peeling bark.

4 Use hand pruners to remove spindly suckers that emerge from the base of the tree. Prune away thin, vertical waterspouts on branches, too.

share space with people and may be necessary to allow more light to reach a planting area below the tree or enable people to pass easily under it. Many trees have striped, patchy, or peeling bark that is obscured by dense branching. By removing the lower branches of these trees, you can expose the bark to year-round enjoyment. ❧Branches that grow low on a tree will always be at that same low height, because trees grow from their tips, gradually elongating at the top, not from their base. If you need to remove the lower branches of a tree, do so when it's young so the wound heals quickly and properly.

trees with attractive trunks

- *Crapemyrtle*
- *Franklinia*
- *Japanese tree clethra*
- *Kousa dogwood*
- *Lacebark elm*
- *Lacebark pine*
- *London planetree*
- *Mexican paloverde*
- *Paperbark maple*
- *Parrotia*
- *River birch*
- *Shagbark hickory*
- *Stewartia*
- *Striped maple*
- *Sycamore*
- *White birch*

5 Groves of trees, such as these 'Heritage' river birches, are limbed-up to show their bark. A bench encourages you to pause and enjoy their beauty.

shaping shrubs

Many shrubs grow rapidly, and in their enthusiasm, they become overgrown, excessively twiggy, and weighted down with excess foliage. This bushiness eventually obscures their structure, reduces flowering, and invites fungal disease. Periodic pruning makes them more attractive and healthier. Pruning to control size is a waste of time—they will just grow back. Instead, guide them so they grow to their mature size with strong stems and healthy foliage. Experienced gardeners usually do their major structural pruning when shrubs are dormant, then perform follow-up shaping during the growing season, after the spring growth spurt. Prune your flowering shrubs to shape them after

dormancy

Whether deciduous or evergreen, trees and shrubs have a dormant period. Except for certain tropical trees, this rest time is usually during the cold winter months. During the period when days are short and the ground is cold, they suspend active growth and live off of stored energy. Warm weather triggers new vitality.

shaping forsythia

1 Overgrown shrubs look unkempt and unattractive and don't bloom well. Thinning the dense foliage-covered branches of this forsythia allows light and air to penetrate and improve its health.

2 The first step is to cut back excessively long branches. Clip them off where a leaf emerges back on the stem near the main mass of foliage. Avoid making them all identical lengths.

3 Reach deep within the dense tangle of branches and clip off particularly large or twiggy ones to the point where they join a main branch.

4 Once its general shape is established, give the shrub a final once-over. Be sure no branches rub against walls or tangle in nearby plants.

they've bloomed and before they set buds for the following year, so you don't inadvertently remove the buds and ruin next year's bloom. Plan to shape spring bloomers, such as rhododendron, azalea, and forsythia, in early to midsummer. Wait to shape summer bloomers, such as crapemyrtle and glossy abelia, until autumn. They form their buds for the new season early in the summer. Clip branches individually, and reserve shearing for hedges. The idea is to groom the shrub to curb unruliness, not to change its appearance. Properly shaped, the shrub should look essentially the same, only neater.

shaping shrubs

When shaping shrubs, get optimum results by honoring their natural habit. Use restraint. Respect the fact that each shrub is genetically programmed for a certain size, profile, and branching pattern. Make cuts that support these features and preserve the essential character of the plant. Lollipop shapes are not attractive on the front lawn. Leave the highly stylized pruning—topiary, pollarding, and bonsai—to the experts.

103

shaping evergreen hedges

1 If the foliage down on the sides of the hedge doesn't get sufficient sunlight, it will die back. Taper the sides of the hedge so that the lower branches are wider than those at the top.

2 To stimulate growth, trim a hedge with hedge shears or electric clippers below the desired height in spring. When you prune later in the season, don't remove all new growth.

shaping boxwood

1 Boxwood shrubs are commonly used as hedges, because they tolerate repeated shearing well. However, when planted individually, they contribute attractive, fine-textured evergreen foliage to the scene. Periodically clip them to neaten their appearance.

2 Use hand pruners, rather than the hedge shears shown here, to clip off individual branches that protrude from the main foliage body of the shrub. Cut the branches at slightly different lengths to avoid creating a round profile.

renovating shrubs

It's easy to take shrubs for granted. Annual and perennial flowers get most of the attention, while the shrubs gradually grow older and bushier. Those that expand by sending up new shoots at ground level develop into wide clumps of increasingly crowded stems. This preponderance of thick, woody stems causes the shrubs to lose vitality and become vulnerable to disease and insect attack. ❡You can save the cost and effort of replacing a valued, otherwise healthy overgrown shrub by using good pruning techniques to revitalize it. Renovation involves cutting the oldest and thickest of the stems down to ground level and removing them. Because most are likely to be

spring growth

Spring is the period of greatest plant growth. When shrubs emerge from dormancy, all systems are go. If stems are cut back to the ground, the new surge of energy will produce replacement shoots that vibrantly arise from the crown of the shrub and give older shrubs a new lease on life.

1 After several years, shrub stems become crowded. Their leaves and flowers are sparser, and they look disheveled. Thin the shrub when it's dormant by removing the oldest and thickest stems.

2 Use long-handled loppers to cut stems up to an inch in diameter. Cut each stem 1 to 2 feet above the ground and remove it. Then there is room to cut the stub properly at ground level.

5 With about ⅓ of the thick, old stems removed, there's plenty of space for this shrub to send up vigorous new replacement shoots.

6 Cut back extra-long stems to normal length. If the leaves have emerged, don't cut them all off, or the shrub may not grow new shoots.

pruning candidates, the basic rule of thumb is to cut out no more than ⅓ of them at one time. This way, the shrub continues to have a presence in the yard. Meanwhile, the pruning stimulates its root system to send up supple, vigorous replacement stems. If done gradually over a period of six years, this process completely renews an old shrub. ❧Some shrubs that respond well to renovation include: lilac, mock orange, quince, deutzia, weigela, privet, barberry, forsythia, bottlebrush buckeye, shrub dogwoods, beautyberry, spirea, bluebeard, rose of Sharon, Japanese kerria, and staghorn sumac.

yearly pruning

You can increase the beauty of certain shrubs, such as red-twigged dogwood, by cutting back all of the stems every year. This stimulates them to send up new shoots. The new young growth may have brilliantly colored bark. Shrubs that bear flowers on new growth, such as butterfly bush, produce more and better flowers.

105

3 A pruning saw comes in handy for stems that are larger than 1 inch in diameter. This narrow, pointed folding saw fits into tight spaces between crowded stems. It also makes a smooth cut.

4 Thorough renovation of long-neglected shrubs requires removal of about ⅓ of the stems each year or two. After six years, the old stems will have been replaced by vigorous new ones.

keeping up appearances

Give shrubs routine maintenance every year, and they will never reach the point that they need thorough renovation. Begin by choosing the correct plant for each site, so that each has sufficient space to grow to its mature size. Don't overfertilize shrubs. If their soil is decent and they are mulched, they won't need granular, slow-acting fertilizer after the first three or four years. Overfertilization encourages excessive growth and bushiness, which restricts their access to light and air. This stresses plants and makes them vulnerable to pest and disease attack. Water shrubs well whenever rainfall is sparse. Most importantly, prune them lightly and regularly as they grow to establish their structure and shape. Thin their foliage branches if necessary. To prevent overcrowding, annually remove obviously aging stems before they become thick and woody. This helps a shrub constantly and gradually regenerate without undergoing a radical renovation pruning. It's particularly important in preserving the uniform look of a hedge year after year.

regional tree & shrub

	Spring	**Summer**

Cool Climates

Spring
- [ ] Prune woody stems of butterfly bush to about 6 inches from the ground.
- [ ] Prune winter-killed canes of hybrid tea roses back to the ground or to live wood.
- [ ] Prune any broken or injured limbs on trees and shrubs. Remove any branches bearing tent caterpillar nests.
- [ ] Begin renovation of overgrown shrubs by pruning 1/3 of the oldest stems.
- [ ] Fertilize trees and shrubs with a granular, slow-acting product.
- [ ] Mulch bare soil over tree and shrub root zones with a 2- to 3-inch layer of organic material.

Summer
- [ ] Prune to shape or renovate spring-flowering trees and shrubs just after they bloom.
- [ ] Prune to train vines, such as wisteria and climbing roses.
- [ ] Prune broken or injured limbs on trees and shrubs.
- [ ] Transplant young annual and perennial plants into the garden.
- [ ] Transplant new shrubs into the yard.
- [ ] Continue to train vines onto their supports.
- [ ] Mow lawns to maintain them at 3 inches tall.
- [ ] Water newly planted trees, shrubs, vines, and groundcovers as needed.

Warm Climates

Spring
- [ ] Prune broken or injured limbs on trees and shrubs.
- [ ] Prune vines to train them and stimulate new growth.
- [ ] Water trees and shrubs as needed.
- [ ] Plant new trees and shrubs.
- [ ] Renew organic mulch under trees and shrubs.

Summer
- [ ] Prune broken or injured limbs on trees and shrubs.
- [ ] Water plants as needed.
- [ ] Regularly examine trees and shrubs for signs of insect infestation.
- [ ] Prune branches with caterpillar tents or signs of borers and other insect pests.

care checklist

Fall

- ❏ Prune broken or injured limbs on trees and shrubs.
- ❏ After frost, partially cut back hybrid tea roses for winter, and mulch them.
- ❏ Plant or transplant trees and shrubs.

Winter

- ❏ Prune broken or injured limbs on trees and shrubs.
- ❏ Sharpen pruners and mower blade. Clean and store tools.
- ❏ Cut branches of early-flowering trees and shrubs (forsythia, flowering quince, crabapple, dogwood, star magnolia) to bring indoors to force bloom ahead of schedule.
- ❏ Prune most hardwood shade trees in late winter. Don't top a tree or head back its limbs.

- ❏ Prune broken or injured limbs on trees and shrubs.
- ❏ Continue to water trees and shrubs as needed.
- ❏ Renew mulch that has decomposed over the summer.
- ❏ Rake leaves or collect pine needles to use as mulch under trees and shrubs.

- ❏ Prune broken or injured limbs on trees and shrubs.
- ❏ Clean and repair tools and equipment.
- ❏ Install or repair irrigation systems.
- ❏ Choose and order mail-order trees and shrubs for early spring planting.
- ❏ In warmest areas, continue to groom plants that aren't dormant.

creating a great front yard

assessing your options

Your front yard is your public face—an extension of your home. It's also a transition zone, easing you, your family, and guests from the outside world into your sheltered, private domain. Good design helps you create an attractive and inviting welcoming area that doesn't require much effort to maintain. It also enhances the value of your property and creates the necessary curb appeal when it's time to sell your home. Think of your yard as a series of outdoor rooms—each with one or more functions, which may include storage, entertainment, circulation (getting from point A to point B), children's play, food production, or beauty. Because front yards typically concentrate on two of these—beauty and

A white, south-facing wall reflects light and heat from the sun onto nearby plantings in summer. Set up trellises or other supports and train vines to climb them to reduce the harsh glare and heat. Their foliage softens and shades the wall.

Using the same shrub repeatedly limits diversity in your yard. Many kinds of shrubs provide color and texture year-round. They also help keep the landscape healthy, because they host lots of different beneficial creatures. Those that bear colorful berries in the fall attract birds, as well.

Grass competes with tree roots for nutrients and water. And whenever you mow close to the tree, you risk injuring the trunk. But if you mulch the area under the tree canopy, you can improve the tree's health. Living mulch—a groundcover planting—is the ideal choice.

circulation—choose a plan that combines both. Keep your options open so you can make changes easily when you decide to redecorate each room. ❦Let your front yard complement the style of your house. The hardscape (permanent, non-plant features) and softscape (plantings) must work well together to create a congenial setting. If your house has a formal look, stick with a more formal front yard, featuring straight paths, symmetrical plantings, and elegant gates and fences. Manicure the planted areas, deliberately prune hedges and shrubs, and concentrate on using green foliage plants throughout.

111

❦Roof overhangs keep rain from foundation plantings. Save time and precious water by planting out from the overhang so they catch the rain.

❦Shrubs that threaten to block windows and walks are problems. Move them to a spot where they're free to grow naturally. Plant dwarf shrubs in the more restricted areas.

❦Many groundcovers spread aggressively by underground runners, encroaching on the lawn and nearby garden beds. Choose types that grow in clumps and spread gradually. Use sturdy edging around beds to restrain the exuberant ones.

❦Save time, energy, and money by limiting high-maintenance lawn areas. In lawn areas, use a premium mixture of grass varieties suited to your climate. Minimize water, herbicide, and pesticide use by mowing the grass about 3 inches high.

assessing your options (cont'd.)

If your house isn't a formal style, let the landscape have a more natural look. Curve the paths and driveways; build gates and fences that have a rustic flair. Make sure other hardscape features have natural elements, such as hewn wood and stone, rather than iron and painted lumber. Choose lots of colorful plants, and spread them around randomly. Carefully plan the circulation of traffic—for people and vehicles. For example, you'll want to install walks in places where people need to walk, build gates wide enough to accommodate machinery and deliveries, and design driveways to suit your family's parking patterns. Use plants and fences to screen utility boxes, outdoor outlets, and hose faucets. Design other planting areas to provide shade where it's needed and outline

Plants in containers dry out quickly in the summer sun. Those in clay pots and containers that are elevated dry out even faster. Place pots where you can conveniently water them daily—perhaps twice a day during hot summer months. Group containers to save work and to create an attractive effect.

Shrubs, such as this azalea, that need acidic soil may fail to thrive near masonry or mortared walls. Over time, rain and snow may cause lime to leach from the wall and enter the soil, reducing its acidity. Add powdered sulfur or aluminum sulfate to correct the balance.

Most plants, especially bulbs, do best in soil that drains well, yet holds moisture. To improve the soil in areas where clay soil is the norm, build a boxed, raised bed over the clay-soil base. Fill it with good soil, amended with lots of organic matter.

the edges of walks to guide visitors. Locate outdoor lighting for safety as well as beauty so it illuminates walks and steps and enhances security near the front door. ❧Be sure to think low maintenance, too. The right plant in the right place copes well without constant pruning, watering, and spraying. Limit lawn size to reduce time, energy, and money spent on herbicides and pesticides. Beds of groundcovers under trees and shrubs save water and protect the soil. A diversity of plants hosts beneficial insects, birds, and other friends that control pest problems.

❧Trees that are too close to the house can cause roof problems. Check periodically to see that branches don't rub the shingles, drop debris, or clog the gutters. Prune back any that threaten.

❧Tree roots must remain at their natural depth in the soil. If you build a planting bed beneath a tree or otherwise change the grade of the property near a tree, don't pile soil over the root zone or against the trunk.

❧Design your yard so you can view the plantings from inside. Check the sight lines from windows before you plant.

❧Perennial plants return year after year, but bloom for a relatively short time. For color in the yard all summer, plant bright annuals, such as geraniums, petunias, coleus, and impatiens, among the permanent shrubs and perennials.

choosing walk materials

It's easy to take walkways for granted, even though they're critical elements of your front yard. They make it work as an outdoor room, a welcoming area, and a transition zone, simultaneously defining an area and carrying people past it. In short, they're the backbone of your front yard—hard at work creating spaces for lawns and gardens and facilitating traffic. If you give them pleasing proportion and use interesting materials to create them, they automatically become a decorative element, as well. ❧But their basic role is to move people, and the guiding principle to consider is "location, location, location." Put walks and paths where people want to travel on their journeys from

walk-design hint

Create a custom look for your walkway by combining different paving materials. Set concrete stepping stones in a bed of colored gravel. Or dress up an asphalt walk by laying worn bricks along its edges. They provide a contrasting color and neater appearance.

❧Concrete "log" pavers resemble the real ones but last much longer. Use them as stepping stones in a garden bed, woodland area, shallow creek, or in an informal walk across your lawn.

❧A light-colored gravel path is more functional than attractive. Placing landscape fabric underneath discourages weeds but still allows water to drain into the soil. Install an edging to control the gravel.

❧Special paints and stains can dress up concrete steps. Coordinate the color with those of the siding and trim.

❧Shell and gravel paths lend a bright, informal feel to the front entrance. Spread them directly over level, firm soil or compacted sand. Though this loose fill is easy and economical to install, it erodes in heavy rains. As a result, you may need to add more occasionally.

place to place. Anticipate the most popular routes. Consider, for example, what the shortest pathway between a car parked in your driveway and the front door is, and the one between your side door and the barbecue area. Before laying down a walk, you might want to define it with stakes and string for a week to see whether people use it or they choose an alternate path. Choose an appropriate style. Straight paths are more efficient, economical, and formal, while curved paths are less formal and more pleasing visually. An incline approaching your house requires special treatment if the grade is steeper than 10%.

Plank paths work especially well over areas where the ground is not level and where water collects. Use pressure-treated wood or other weather-resistant lumber such as redwood or cedar.

Wood chips are soft underfoot and easy to lay down quickly. Eventually the wood decomposes, requiring a new layer of fresh chips.

A brick walk is durable, elegant, and easy to maintain. Lay it—in one of many patterns—over a base of sand or mortar. Use a complementary edging.

choosing walk materials (cont'd.)

Use steps or a curve to ease the problem. Ramps work, too, and are especially helpful for those who have mobility difficulties. Proportion and scale are important in the design of a walkway—it shouldn't dominate the landscape. Make the walkway as wide as the steps or landing to the house at that point, even if it's narrower earlier in its route. Narrow walks slow people down; use them in gardens where you want guests to linger and enjoy the views. A wide walk is utilitarian and moves people faster, so it's suitable for the main thoroughfare in front of your house. Typically, front walks are 36 to 54 inches wide. Make them—and the structures alongside them, such as arbors—at least wide enough to accommodate two people walking abreast, one

discouraging weeds from walkways

One of the problems with walkways made of loose material, such as wood chips, pebbles, nut hulls, or pine needles, is that weeds can penetrate them. Discourage perennial weeds by laying down landscape fabric first. It allows water to penetrate into the soil but blocks emerging weeds. Then pour at least 2 inches of the loose material over the fabric.

walks

A red-brick path coordinates well with the somewhat formal look of the straight picket fence that runs parallel to it. The path's color sets off the pink plants that spill out of the bed.

Organic material, such as ground or shredded bark, makes a good walking surface for small paths that meander through informal planting areas. Any leftover material may be used to mulch the plants.

stairway planting

This rock garden—fashioned from a stone stairway—is a perfect example of the functional and attractive fusion of hardscape and softscape. To duplicate this design, buy or collect several large pieces of natural stone. Set them in the soil so they'll be stable underfoot. Be sure to have some friends with strong backs help you move them. Then tuck lots of low-maintenance plants—ones that don't need special soil, generous water, or constant grooming—into the spaces between levels to soften the harsh edges of the stone and dot the area with color and texture. The result is a natural garden that harmonizes beautifully with its surroundings.

person carrying a bag of groceries in each arm, or an individual in a wheelchair. Opt for the narrow end of this range if your property is small, the house is narrow, or the distance to the front door is quite short. Be sure that it's sturdy, non-slip, and as level as possible. Use edging to give all of your walks a finished look. A firm edge also keeps the sides of your walks from being damaged. And if the edging material is a contrasting color or pattern, it also helps guide the eye of visitors and keeps them from straying off to the side. Set any decorative fencing at least a foot from the edge of the walk or driveway.

edging

Bricks, in various colors and sizes, create crisp, finished edges along walkways. Experiment with them: Try them on edge, on end, or at an angle. You can use them to edge planted beds, too.

Wood edging continues the informal style and color of a walk that features log stepping stones. Use wood that's decay-resistant. Drive stakes into the soil every few feet to keep the wood from moving.

Concrete edging is similar to curbing, except that it's usually narrower. Install this durable and inconspicuous edge the same way you would curbs.

Plastic edging and similar products made from recycled car tires or other materials will last many years. Some are available in several colors.

using walls & fences

Walls and fences can be significant hardscape elements of your yard. Because one of their main functions is to define space, they literally can create a front yard for you by carving out a private space and separating it from the public world. In the process, they contribute character and beauty to your entire landscape. Of course, the purpose of a wall or fence influences its design. One common use is to establish a degree of privacy from the public. This is especially important if your property fronts a busy street, or if the neighboring houses crowd you. Design is critical in these cases. Typically, privacy fences are 6 feet tall. A fence along property lines taller than that or a stockade or other

weather

Weather takes its toll on fences. Humidity creates rust on iron and mildew and decay on wood. Harsh sun causes paint to peel. Soil heaved by frost loosens posts and topples rails. So be sure to use sturdy materials and solid construction techniques to keep your upkeep to a minimum.

This picket fence features narrow slats with wider than usual spacing. The more open style gives the fence a light, airy feeling and permits a clear view of the plants on the other side.

Wooden gates set in an imposing stone wall make an attractive contrast. The design is strong enough to blend well with the stone yet light enough to relieve the massiveness of the wall.

Ornamental gates add elegance to virtually any style of fence or wall. Buy one from a supplier, or design and build your own.

Most municipalities require that you surround a swimming pool with a security fence. There's no reason it can't be attractive as well as utilitarian.

solid-surface fence, although a more effective screen, sends a negative message and is often regarded as a spite fence. Check with local authorities to determine height restrictions, if any. As you plan your front yard, you may want to temper your inclination for privacy with the desire to present a welcoming view. You can do this by using walls or fences that are only about 4 feet high or that have open spaces, like picket, split-rail, and wrought-iron fences. They still delimit boundaries and offer an inviting glimpse inside, while, at the same time, they discourage shortcuts across your lawn.

Rustic fences have a country charm. Use materials at hand, such as the unpainted scrap wood shown here or bare branches of willow or other trees. They don't have to be a uniform width.

A wattle fence made of kudzu, grape, or other flexible, woody plant stems encloses beds as it simultaneously showcases low-growing plants.

An unpainted picket fence requires much less maintenance than a painted one. Here the rustic color harmonizes with the siding on the house.

using walls & fences (cont'd.)

Openings in fences and walls are especially important if they enclose—or serve as a border for—plantings of any kind. They admit light and encourage good airflow that keep flowers and shrubs from overheating or developing mildew. ❧Fences and walls separate the children's play area or the dog's territory from the main yard. They establish space for specialty gardens or for a sheltered microclimate for certain plants such as edibles. Specially designed fences keep undesirable wildlife out of vegetable patches. And many types of walls and fences support plants that like to climb and ramble. Roses covering a fence—or plants growing from the cracks in a stone wall—soften their architectural lines and help them blend into the surrounding softscape. ❧Build your walls

gates

Gates are decorative features as well as practical devices that provide passageways through a fence or wall. Choose interesting designs that coordinate with the style of your fence. Locate them in places that are convenient; gates don't necessarily have to accompany a walkway. The longer you make the fence or wall—or the larger the area it encloses—the more gates you'll need.

❧The charming design of an arbored entry gate combines with the beautiful plants it frames to create a doubly ornamental entrance.

❧A fence with mirrors mounted in strategic places opens up a limited space and adds an element of fun and whimsy to a yard or garden. The mirrors reflect extra light and create a sense of depth.

❧Brick or stone walls give any yard a sense of permanence and security. Cutouts in the wall encourage air circulation and add a decorative touch.

and fences with materials that complement those of the house. Use native stone or weather-resistant wood from trees indigenous to the region to add character and a sense of place to the landscape. If you opt for a brick wall—and your house has a brick exterior—make sure the wall brick matches that of the house. Proportion is important, too. If you plan to parallel a walk or path with a new wall or fence, limit its height to no more than 2 feet so you can maintain a sense of space, as well as allow room for swinging arms. And keep it at least 2 feet away from the traffic path to avoid a crowded effect.

Bamboo fencing is particularly appropriate for Asian-themed yards and gardens but is also practical and adaptable for other areas. Its relatively fine-textured format provides good privacy screening.

There's nothing more classic than a white picket fence surrounding a garden or the entire property. It sets off the colors and textures of all kinds of plants and gives them good air circulation.

Fenced screens partition rather than enclose an area. This white, airy structure is decorative—with or without a colorful cover of climbing plants.

Living wall of plants

Prune a row of shrubs to create a living wall. Hedges make useful and attractive enclosures for yards or gardens. Their foliage absorbs sound and provides a soft backdrop for colorful gardens. Those made of thorny shrubs are also very effective barriers.

a great entryway

Entryways are opportunities for gardens. What better way to welcome guests than with plants? One of the loveliest and longest traditions in old cities and rural areas is to use plants to soften and enhance the architectural lines of utilitarian walkways, steps, railings, and front doors. For city homes, a windowbox full of pansies or a pot of geraniums on the *front stoop* effectively produces a garden atmosphere. In the country, families often greet their guests with a personalized *dooryard*—typically an area filled with an entertaining jumble of flowering plants or herbs that's enclosed by a picket fence, low wall, or arbor over which roses ramble. ❧Until recently, most

plant placement

Put plants where they won't get in the way when you need to work on the exterior of your house. Keep shrubs away from the foundation so the outdoor faucet and electrical outlets are always accessible. Train climbing plants on trellises so you can reach steps, railings, and siding to repair and repaint them.

☙A climbing rose over the door suggests the informality of rural life. Add annual vines to provide continual color after the roses have faded.

☙Containers full of brightly colored flowers and foliage welcome guests. Strategic placement of the flowers warns visitors about steps and landings.

homeowners in the exurbs and suburbs overlooked the potential of the space approaching the front door as a garden area. Big expanses of high-maintenance green lawn, dotted with the occasional island of groundcover, sweep practically to the front door. And, almost uniformly, you'll still find row upon row of evergreen shrubs, originally intended to hide the concrete of the poured foundation where it emerges above the soil surface. Unfortunately, many of these serviceable shrubs invariably survive to grow as tall as the house—or at least high enough to cover the front windows. This brings visibility and

Low-growing flowers spill onto this stepping-stone entry walk. The color and foliage soften the edges of the walk and provide a cheerful greeting.

a great entryway (cont'd.)

security problems. However, things are changing in the suburbs and exurbs. These days, the approach to the front door is called an *entryway* (or *front courtyard*, if it's tucked between the front entrance and a garage that protrudes from the front of the house). Along with the change in name is a change in perception. Owners are suddenly appreciating this area for its potential as an outdoor room—or, more accurately, an outdoor foyer. Why not develop this entryway into an area that will decorate the house and welcome visitors? Plant a garden there. Replace the tired shrubs and lots of lawn around the front

using edibles as ornamentals

One way to make the entryway doubly useful is to plant vegetables there. An edible landscape can be as colorful and varied as a flower garden. Plant vines (tomatoes and scarlet runner beans), ground covers (red and green lettuces), shrubby plants (peppers, red cabbage, and white, purple, or striped eggplant), and containers full of herbs. The result is a garden that's as tasty as it is ornamental.

This neat flagstone walk is flanked by large, sheltering trees. The impatiens, azaleas, and ferns nestling in their shade make the approach to the house a delightful walk in the woods.

walk with lively plants that look better and take less care than grass does. Add hardscape features, such as paths, lighting, raised beds, steps, and terraces, to showcase them. Use traditional annual and perennial flowers, plus bulbs and a small ornamental tree or two if there's enough space. Plant ornamental grasses or evergreen and flowering vines. Hang baskets of flowers from the lamppost or porch. If the area has the best sun on the property, put the rose garden or the vegetable garden there.

This new walkway defines a perfect area for planting ornamental plants that like sun. The color and texture of the bright flowers draw visitors' eyes away from the newness of the walk.

Successful entryways reflect the style of the home. This geometric walkway and the linear rows of small shrubs alongside it echo the clean lines and straight edges of this contemporary house.

Here, the approach to a traditional home is lined with period plantings, including hostas, ivy, and impatiens. Ferns in hanging baskets soften the architectural lines of the porch and are welcoming.

suit the planting to the site

The most attractive entry gardens are those that blend best with the style and scale of the home. And those that also take into account the conditions that exist on the site are destined to be the most successful. Plants look their best and are healthiest when they're happy—free from stress and the factors that cause it. Choose plants that will be happy in the soil and in the light around the entrance to your home. Consider the exposure. The area around a south-facing front door will get heated up by the harsh sun during the summer, and that heat will be intensified by reflections from nearby paving. Choose plants that like sun and don't need constant watering. Plant a small tree or two to create some shade for plants as well as visitors. Consider your soil, too. If it's clay or sand, choose plants that can cope with these difficult soils. It's considerably easier to change the plant than to change the soil.

outdoor lighting

Today, lighting the yard is much more than turning on the outdoor light so visitors can see their way to the door at night. While these lights are still important for safety and security, they're only part of the story. Thanks to technology, most families can afford to buy low-voltage landscape lighting. It extends outdoor living on the deck or patio well into the night and makes plants glow dramatically after sundown. On winter nights, this system marks the walkways and highlights the beautiful landscape. Low-voltage outdoor lighting is powered by regular 115-volt household current, but it's channeled through a transformer that reduces it to 12 volts—so weak it won't shock you even if you

light sensitivity

Some trees are sensitive to night lighting, especially bright streetlights. If lights are on every night, all night, they may disrupt the growth cycle of basswood, birch, black locust, catalpa, cottonwood, dogwood, elm, goldenrain tree, hemlock, honeylocust, maple, redbud, silverbell, sumac, sycamore, and zelkova.

safety lighting

Low-voltage accent lights along the walk help augment the front-door light. And during rainstorms, the low-placed fixtures highlight puddles and slippery spots to improve the safety of family and guests.

These low-voltage accent lights reveal the uneven texture in this paving at night. The cheery yellow marigolds, which brighten the walk during the day, reflect the lights' glow after dark.

Low-voltage post lights do a good job of illuminating potential hazards, such as high curbs, changes in grade, and steps. This light keeps nighttime walkers from running into the corner of a raised garden bed. Note that the fixture is placed inside, rather than outside, the bed to avoid lawn mower or weeder damage.

Rectangular deck lights recess snugly between the railing posts in this installation. You could move the mounting point lower to direct the light closer to the railing, or place it at the top to spread the light farther out onto the decking. A small light on the end post calls attention to the transition to steps.

touch the bare wires. Also, you don't need to bury the wires that connect the light fixtures. Just hide them under some mulch or string them along a railing or fence. They're easy to install, and a set of six lights costs only pennies a day to operate, even if you use them 12 hours at a stretch. ❧Design the

two types of lighting

Downlighting from capped fixtures, called tiered or mushroom lights, casts a soft glow. It lights the walk for safety and accents the nearby groundcover. Because it's directed downward from a low position, the light doesn't dissipate the darkness enough to compromise night vision.

Deck lighting casts light downward onto stairs to ensure safe passage at night. You can easily install the fixtures by stapling their cables onto the wooden risers or along the base of the railing.

These deck lights clearly indicate the change in height from one railing to the next and signal a corner and grade change.

Most uplighting is for effect. Strategically placed flood or spotlights illuminate special features of the landscape such as a specimen shade tree or statue. The resulting shadows make their own contribution to the nighttime scene. Use uplighting sparingly to avoid creating distractions.

outdoor lighting (cont'd.)

placement of your landscape lighting fixtures with three thoughts in mind—security, safety, and beauty. To increase security and safety around your property, use unobtrusive fixtures that direct their light downward along walks and steps. The lights cast a glow that defines a walkway or driveway and reveals any potential hazards such as surface roots, planted containers, fallen branches, children's toys, or patches of ice or gravel. Position floodlights to illuminate dark areas in groves of trees or among shrubs, where an intruder might hide. Some sets include motion-detector lights with infrared sensors. Use these to light the driveway and property boundaries. They turn on automatically when anyone approaches the house on foot or by car after dark. To enhance the

siting electrical outlets

If you plan to set up low-voltage lights in several areas of the yard, install outdoor electrical outlets on each side of the house. This arrangement will give you more flexibility and save you money on cable. You'll need a transformer for each outlet.

decorative lighting

Once you have the low-voltage equipment, you can personalize or modify the lights. A California gardener shows off his seashell collection by mounting them on stakes with low-voltage lights.

Illuminating the garden with electric lights doesn't have a long history. In fact, the first garden to be lighted at night was in East Hampton, New York in 1916. Old fixtures are highly collectible.

This oversized streetlamp uses a conventional light bulb, but it's a real eye-catcher, nevertheless. It's on a pedestal, surrounded by cannas.

Flower-shaped fixtures are certainly appropriate to downlight a garden path at night. During the day, they nod unobtrusively above their plant companions.

beauty of your yard after dark, place fixtures as if you were painting with light. Experiment with post lights, accent lights, and floodlights. Create a mood by carefully locating fixtures around planted beds, under vines and trees, and in or near a water feature. Showcase special plants, dramatize bark and foliage texture, and create exotic shadows. Because low-voltage lights accent the features of the subject they are lighting, rather than draw attention to themselves, most are made of black polymer plastic. Exceptions are higher-end Chinese lanterns and other stylized or antique fixtures that are ornamental day and

Although most lights used for safety and security are unobtrusive, others, like this mission-style lantern, add a decorative touch during the day and complement the style and flavor of the garden.

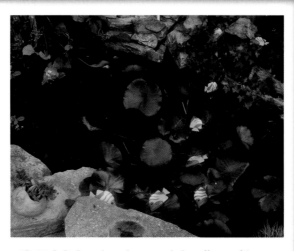

Fish lights cleverly extend the effects of low-voltage lighting to water-garden areas. Special fixtures can set all kinds of moods, create drama or mystery, encourage reflection, or just introduce whimsy.

Lanterns are naturals for garden light fixtures. They're sturdy and weatherproof, and you can mount them easily on posts, fences, and railings.

seat yourself

Lighting along a garden path conducts you safely through it at night. However, fixtures that accent plants, water, and ornaments—and make pale flowers glow luminously—encourage you to stay and enjoy the mood. Be sure to include a comfortable seat so you can pause to enjoy the special experience that is a garden after dark. Lighting reveals the magnificent moths visiting moonflowers and yucca at night. Its reflection on water, and the shadows it casts on walls and walks, change the entire character of the garden.

outdoor lighting (cont'd.)

night. Depending on their design, low-voltage fixtures emit light in slightly different ways. You can configure them to produce any of these three effects: downlighting, uplighting, and sidelighting. *Downlighting* imitates nature, illuminating items from above. Flood or spotlights mounted high in trees, on posts, or under roof eaves cast light downward, as the moon would, to create a pale glow in the garden or on the lawn or pool. *Uplighting* creates a more

dramatic effect. The same flood or spotlights positioned on the ground—but aimed upward—can give gnarled tree branches, statuary, and special architectural features a stark relief. *Sidelighting* emphasizes details. Because the light is softer, it doesn't cast such harsh shadows. Set lights on two

lighting tips

A little lighting goes a long way. That's the principle behind the two major rules of landscape lighting: (1) Don't overdo the lighting in your yard. The result will be confusing and garish. (2) Take pains to ensure that your lighting doesn't disturb your neighbors. Sometimes it shines into nearby windows or eliminates darkness that neighbors prefer.

decorative lighting

Have some fun with your landscape lighting. Use accent fixtures as features in and of themselves. Deliberately overdo small areas for effect. Colored panes increase the options for unconventional decor.

Fixtures that downlight have covers over the bulb that simultaneously direct the light toward the ground and prevent it from escaping upward to cause glare in people's eyes. In this installation, form follows function as the drooping petals of this decorative flower-light fixture cast their glow onto the plants and path below.

Globe lights are very versatile. When you mount them overhead, they do an excellent job of lighting a walk for the safety of those using it after dark. And when you use them individually as accent lights in areas throughout your property, their full-moon shape and soft glow create an other-world mood.

The manufacturer of these wall blocks/pavers produces matching blocks with low-voltage lighting embedded within them to produce a subtle glow.

or more sides of the feature you want to light so their beams merge as they pass over the object for a three-dimensional effect. A fourth term called *grazing* refers to a procedure you can use with the three types of lighting effects. As the name implies, you aim a fixture so its beam of light just skims the subject. For example, highlight the surface textures of tree bark or rough stucco by stretching the light all across the surface to make it glow. Before installing a set of lights, connect them and lay them out on the ground. Then try them after dark to find out whether they create the effect you want.

Underwater lights—encased in waterproof mounts and professionally installed—add a special dimension to a water garden or pool. This installation accents the waterfall for nighttime visitors.

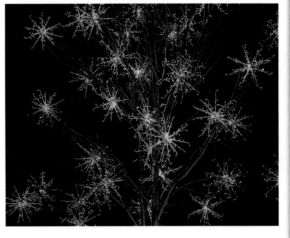

Sparkle lights strung on trees, deck railings, and other supports immediately cheer up a nocturnal scene. Most familiar at Christmastime, they bring their same fairyland beauty to a summer landscape.

These portable novelty flower lights are powered by batteries in their hollow plastic stems. Just twist the blossom to light the bulb in the center.

You can create your own decorative fixtures in a variety of styles from recycled objects. These are made from an upside-down can and a shell.

yard basics

climate: understanding

Plants grow most successfully when they are adapted to the climate where they are planted. Based on measurements of the lowest recorded temperatures across the country, the United States Department of Agriculture has designated a series of geographic climate zones. They are numbered 1 to 11, coldest to warmest. ¶When you shop for perennials, shrubs, or trees, check the plant tags to determine whether they can tolerate winter in your zone. The tags usually indicate a cold-hardiness range by listing two numbers. If there's only one number, it identifies the coldest area where the plant will survive winter.

Local garden centers and nurseries should carry those plants that are suited to the local climate. ¶Your property has microclimates—small pockets where prevailing temperatures vary—often within a few yards of each other. Near the house, which offers shelter and radiates heat, conditions are warmer—by as much as one zone—than slopes that experience harsh wind and sun. Be aware of these variations when siting your plants.

USDA hardiness zone map

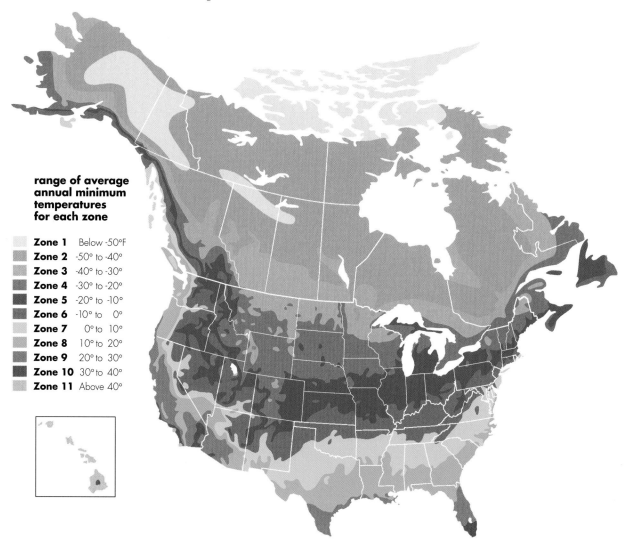

**range of average
annual minimum
temperatures
for each zone**

	Zone 1	Below -50°F
	Zone 2	-50° to -40°
	Zone 3	-40° to -30°
	Zone 4	-30° to -20°
	Zone 5	-20° to -10°
	Zone 6	-10° to 0°
	Zone 7	0° to 10°
	Zone 8	10° to 20°
	Zone 9	20° to 30°
	Zone 10	30° to 40°
	Zone 11	Above 40°

your zone

spring frost dates

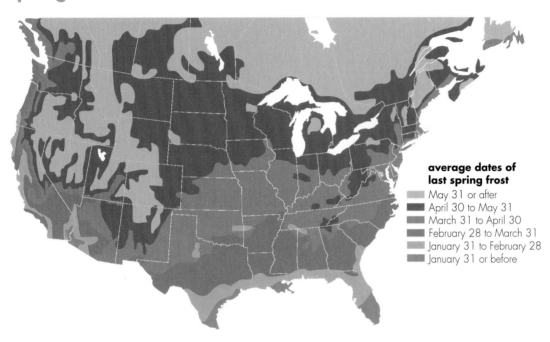

average dates of last spring frost

- May 31 or after
- April 30 to May 31
- March 31 to April 30
- February 28 to March 31
- January 31 to February 28
- January 31 or before

autumn frost dates

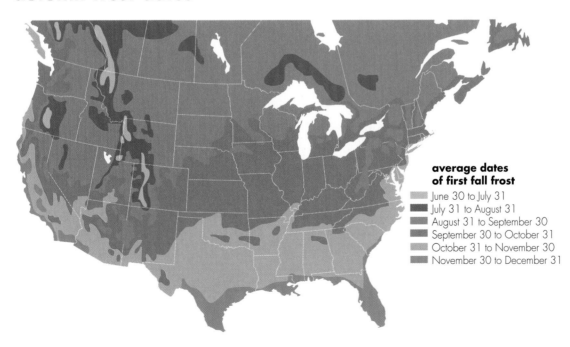

average dates of first fall frost

- June 30 to July 31
- July 31 to August 31
- August 31 to September 30
- September 30 to October 31
- October 31 to November 30
- November 30 to December 31

yard & garden tools

There is no denying that gardening is hard physical work. But it's *pleasurable* hard work, made all the easier by good-quality, appropriate tools. Just a few basic tools, well-designed for comfort and carefully crafted from the best materials, will serve in most situations. If you care for them properly, they should last a lifetime. When purchasing tools, always choose quality over quantity. Today's tools are ergonomically designed to spare backs, shoulders, and wrists. Space-age materials make them lighter, more balanced, and easier to grip and use without developing calluses. Look for tools with features such as replaceable parts,

garden spade

A spade is not the same tool as a shovel. A spade is short-handled and has a flat, squared-off blade. It is ideal for edging beds, digging planting holes, slicing under sod, and working soil amendments into the garden. In a pinch you can even use a spade to chop ice on walks. Its versatility makes it a staple in the tool shed.

garden fork

Dig into the soil with the four straight, sturdy steel tines of a garden fork. Also known as a spading fork, it's a good tool for turning and aerating the soil. Use it to break up chunks of soil and to work organic matter, fertilizer, and other amendments into the soil. A garden fork copes easily with occasional buried roots or rocks and comes in handy for dividing clumps of perennials.

shovel

A garden shovel typically has a dished (concave) blade that is rounded or mildly tapered at the tip. Most shovels are long-handled, although you can buy them with short handles, too. Because the blade is canted at an angle to the handle for greater leverage, a shovel is ideal for attacking piles of soil, sand, and other materials you need to load or move.

hoe

Cultivate the soil and remove young weeds in a garden bed with a hoe. The simplest hoe is basically a straight-edged, square blade attached at a right angle to a long wooden handle. It's useful for chopping clumps of soil and scraping the soil surface to cut off sprouting weeds. When tilted at an angle, the corner of the blade traces neat planting furrows in prepared soil. There are many different types of hoes. A swan hoe has a curved neck. A diamond hoe has a head that is diamond-shaped, perfect for pulling weeds from between plants.

easy cleaning, rust-proof metal parts, and a hole in handles so you can hang the tool on a peg. ❦Try out tools in the store before you buy them. Check out their grips to make sure they will be comfortable after repeated use. Good pruners, for example, come in different sizes to fit your grip—you want ones with handles that don't open wider than your hand. For hoes, handle length is important—it should come up to nose height. Hold the hoe upright and use only your hands and forearms to move it forward and backward. This means no bending—and no backache!

steel rake

Also called a garden rake, this tool features 12 or 14 short steel tines mounted on a sturdy steel bridge at the end of a long handle. Use a steel rake to dress and smooth out prepared soil in a planting bed. Its tines simultaneously break up small clods of soil and corral stones and debris. Use a flathead style to level the soil for planting. Flip the rake over so its bridge scrapes along the surface of the soil.

flexible rake

The business end of this type of rake, sometimes called a lawn or leaf rake, is a fan of flat, flexible tines. Typically bent at their tips, the tines are made of lengths of metal, bamboo, plastic, or even rubber in a variety of styles. The tines are attached to a long handle for easy control. Use a flexible rake to gather light debris that is spread out on beds, lawns, and walks, and to rake up leaves.

trowel

The basic hand tool for digging, a trowel is indispensable for planting bulbs, seedlings, and other small plants in a garden bed. Trowels are available with sturdy handles and narrow or wide, cupped metal blades with tapered tips. Different sizes—widths and lengths—suit different planting jobs.

hand weeder

This tool is basically a miniature hoe, which most gardeners use for down-and-dirty weeding. The short handle at the end of a flat, straight-edged blade allows you to maneuver between plants in a bed. The blade may be square or triangular and mounted at various angles for flexibility. Position the blade on the soil and draw it toward you to cut weeds off at—or just below—the soil level. Or turn the blade upward, so its corner digs deeper to dislodge stones or pry out larger weeds.

yard & garden tools (cont'd.)

Some essential gardening and yard care equipment doesn't always fall into the traditional tool category. However, they are as useful and labor-saving as familiar tools such as shovels and pruners. Watering devices, gardening garb, and equipment to carry things are included into this group. So are storage facilities and maintenance tools from your household tool kit. They increase your efficiency and safety as you care for the plants in your yard and the power tools that help you with these tasks. Even what you wear while doing yard work is important. Protective clothing with long sleeves and long pants, and devices such as safety glasses and ear protectors, are essential. Remember to wear a hat and sunscreen to protect your skin from harmful rays of the sun. Pay

preventing hearing loss

Repeated and long-term exposure to noise causes progressive hearing loss. Even sound that is not terribly loud can gradually impair your hearing over many years. Wear ear protection when you use any power equipment for more than 10 minutes. Ear protectors that are designed for shooting ranges offer the best protection.

watering can

Because water is crucial to the well-being of plants, the watering can is an old standby. Originally made from galvanized metal—and now in a variety of materials from brass to plastic—it retains its classic form. A bucket-like reservoir that holds the water is flanked with a bowed handle on one side. On the opposite side, a long spout capped with a sprinkler head, or rose, protrudes. Choose a can that feels balanced when full and holds a generous amount of water without straining your arms as you carry it.

hose

A hose is indispensable for maintaining plants in any yard or garden larger than a few square feet. At every life stage, plants need water for good health, and a hose at the ready can bridge periods of scant rainfall. Buy the best hose your budget will allow. Choose a rubber or vinyl hose constructed of several layers of mesh and with sturdy connectors to ensure long life. It will save you from carrying a watering can during hot weather.

watering tools — hose attachments

A **nozzle**, which used to be made of brass and now comes in a variety of materials, sizes, and shapes—is essential to control the stream of water coming out of the hose. A **watering wand**, a long tube extension with a sprinkler head at the tip, converts the hose to a long-distance watering can. Use it to water containers, hanging pots, and beds. The wand should have a shutoff at its connection to the hose to prevent wasting water. Another key tool is a **sprinkler**, which you attach to the hose and place on the ground. It oscillates or rotates to deliver water to beds and lawns. The best sprinklers have timers and adjustments for the width and direction of the stream.

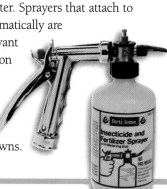

sprayers

Fertilizers, tonics, fungicides, insecticidal soaps, and many other products are water-soluble and most effective if sprayed on plant foliage. Although many are packaged ready-to-use in spray bottles, they are more economical if you buy them in concentrated form that you mix in water. Sprayers that attach to the hose and dilute automatically are convenient. You might want to have a one- or two-gallon pump sprayer for small jobs. Larger backpack units are useful for spraying fertilizer over broader areas such as lawns.

particular attention to sensitive skin areas such as the back of your neck and your ears. Be sure to protect your feet with sturdy shoes. They will prevent injury from equipment, as well as properly support your legs and back. Non-skid soles, found on athletic shoes and rubber gardening shoes or boots, reduce the danger of slipping on wet grass or ice. Wear heavy work boots when working with a chainsaw, log splitter, or similar equipment. And whenever you use a ladder, wear non-skid shoes or boots that are flexible enough to allow you to negotiate the steps safely.

safety glasses

Special glasses made from sturdy plastic are a must. Choose from various styles that feature wrap-around lenses to protect eyes from flying objects while mowing, sawing, chopping, or tilling. Some models are designed to fit over prescription eyeglasses. Others may be tinted for work in the sun or may be attached to a hard hat for construction or arbor work. Be sure they fit snugly over your ears to prevent slipping.

gloves

Different types of gloves protect hands from different injuries. Have several pairs available for yard-care tasks. Choose leather or cloth gloves to avoid blisters from repetitive tasks such as sawing, pruning, and shoveling. Wide-cuffed or long gloves coated with nitrile or plastic protect wrists and forearms when you're working with thorny plants. Latex or rubber gloves protect against soil-borne fungi that cause dermatitis. Check the fit by making a fist, then feel for finger fit at the tips of the glove fingers.

wheelbarrows, carts, wagons

Yards and gardens generate a lot of debris that you need to transport to the compost pile. They also benefit from the loads of organic matter and mulch you haul in and distribute. Garden carts and wheelbarrows do these jobs and many others. Use a stable, two-wheeled cart with high sides for large, bulky loads. It can handle up to 500 pounds on its pneumatic tires. The smaller, nimbler wheelbarrow —available in one- or two-wheel models—is easier to maneuver around small spaces.

kneelers and seats

While one of the many attractions of gardening is the opportunity to kneel down close to the soil, getting up gracefully afterward can become a problem as age takes its toll on your knees and back. Kneelers of various kinds cushion the contact with the hard ground. Those that have a metal frame with tall side bars also help you stand up afterward. Low gardening seats— either on metal frames or on wheeled tool carts—also ease back and knee strain. Some knee pads strap on over pants to protect your knees and keep your pants clean.

lawn-care tools

Lawns are high-maintenance landscape features. However, for those of us who grew up with front and back yards covered with grass, it's difficult to imagine not having at least some lawn. Nothing equals grass as a soft place for children to tumble and play and as a rich green backdrop to showcase landscape plantings. That beautiful surface of emerald green is greedy for water, fertilizer, your time, and energy. That means regular mowing, edging, repairing, aerating, and topdressing. Homeowners with small lawns—under 4,000 square feet—can accomplish most of these maintenance jobs with a small assortment of hand tools. If you prefer the quiet and enjoy the exercise,

weather

For the healthiest grass and most uniform cut, mow the lawn when it is dry. When it is damp with early-morning dew or wet from rainfall, blades don't cut cleanly and clippings clump. Any existing fungal disease will be tracked onto healthy lawn areas.

power lawn mower

A gasoline- or electric-powered rotary lawn mower is appropriate for lawns over 4,000 square feet. If the lawn is configured as a large expanse, self-propelled models are particularly helpful. Today almost all power lawn mowers are designed as mulching mowers with a special blade and higher bell that suspends clippings long enough to be cut several times before they fall back into the grass as a mulch. There's no need to collect them.

drop spreader

Use a drop spreader to sow grass seed, lime, or granular fertilizer precisely. The granules or seeds flow from a rectangular hopper in measured amounts in a row along its wheelbase. An adjustment on the handle alters the amount you dispense. With each pass across the lawn, this spreader evenly distributes the material in spreader-width rows. It's perfect for lawns with straight edges but requires a careful pattern of passes so you don't leave any missed strips.

rotary spreader

Rotary spreaders broadcast seed or granular fertilizer in a wide, circular pattern. When you push the spreader, a spinner—under the hopper that holds the material—rotates, throwing out the seed or granules at a rate regulated by a lever on the handle. Because the spreader casts the material widely on both sides of it, there's no danger of missing areas that show later as streaks in the lawn. To ensure uniform coverage, make vertical and horizontal passes over the area.

manual (reel) mower

The old-fashioned lawn mower has been updated for modern times. It's now made of lightweight space-age materials—most models feature pneumatic tires, easy blade-height settings, and handle-length adjustment. The horizontal blades on this type of mower always have given a superior cut. They are mounted on a reel that's geared within the wheel assembly, and they slice the grass against a lower, rigid bar. Spectacularly quiet and, of course, pollution-free, these manual mowers are especially useful for smaller lawns.

hand tools also will save money. A manual mower, broadcast seeder, edger, and aerating tool work just fine. Use a lawn rake to spread organic material for topdressing in the fall or spring, and use hand grass clippers to clean up weedy patches along walls and fences. Medium lawns—4,000 to 10,000 square feet—are generally too extensive for hand tools. A powered rotary mulching mower is faster, and a self-propelled version is easier. Fall mowings with this type of mower also provide your lawn with an organic topdressing—chopped leaves—if you have deciduous trees on your property.

hand edger

A hand edger consists of a sharp, straight-edged steel blade mounted at the end of a long wooden or Fiberglass handle. This English-style version has a rounded semicircular blade with a broad top edge that forms a tread for your foot. Place the tool along the edge of the turf where it meets pavement, then push the blade downward to cut a neat border.

dethatching rake

The steel tines on this special rake penetrate the thatch layer on a lawn. They are mounted on a sturdy bridge that's attached to a long wooden handle. When you pull the tines through the grass with a raking motion, they snag the matted strands of dead grass plants that make up the thatch layer. They bypass the healthy grass and loosen and pull up only dead material. On some models, you can adjust the angle of the row of tines.

electric-powered edger

For edging long stretches of lawn along walks and driveways, a powered edger is most efficient. If you have a large property or a lot of lawn that you want to keep perfectly edged, this tool's for you. Electric-powered edgers are available in corded and battery-powered models. Before choosing one, consider the length the electric cord would have to be to reach the nearest electrical outlet from the farthest area you will be edging. When using a powered edger, you want to be aware of where any shallowly buried electric or water lines may lie—a consideration if you have an in-ground irrigation system for the lawn. You don't want to cut any lines accidentally.

hand core-aerator

Hand core-aerators consist of two or more hollow tines connected by a narrow, steel bridge that serves as a foot plate. A waist-high, steel handle, topped by hand grips, attaches to the bridge. When you press your foot against the steel bridge, the 6-inch-long tines penetrate moist turf and fill up with a core of soil. Then when you withdraw them, each one leaves a narrow hole in the turf that admits air and moisture to the root area. Each time you press the tines into the turf, a soil plug pops out the top and lands on the lawn where it decomposes in the rain.

lawn-care tools (cont'd.)

On medium-sized lawns, you're better off renting a power core-aerating machine to aerate properly. Lawns of this scale are likely to have many more feet of edges to manicure, so a powered edger is a good idea, too. Use power string-trimmers to clean up weeds around fence posts and walls. ❧Large lawns—over 10,000 square feet—require even more sophisticated equipment. A large powered rotary mulching mower can do the job, but a riding mower may be more appropriate. The powered core-aerator, edger, and weed trimmer are essential. ❧Whatever the lawn size and whichever the tools, choose them carefully,

lawn mower troubleshooting checklist

If the lawn mower doesn't start, ask yourself:

❏ *Is there gas in the tank?*

❏ *Is the starter switch on or the baffle engaged?*

❏ *Have you primed the engine?*

❏ *Is the spark plug old or disconnected?*

❏ *Is anything obstructing the blade?*

❏ *Is last season's gas still in it?*

❏ *If it has an electric motor, is the cord plugged in?*

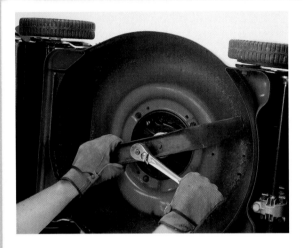

1 To sharpen the mower blade, disconnect the spark plug or unplug the mower. Then turn the mower over and remove the nut that attaches the blade to the motor.

2 Stabilize the blade in a vise and use a medium file to smooth out imperfections along the blade edge (at the ends of mulching blades). Don't try to hone a sharp edge.

3 After you smooth the cutting edge on both halves of the blade, check to see if the blade is balanced. If not, remove more metal from one of the halves until the blade does balance.

bagging attachments

In most cases, it's best to allow your grass clippings to fall onto the lawn rather than collect in a mower bag attachment. Mulching blades on modern power rotary mowers chop clippings into tiny pieces that fall among the grass blades and give the lawn a little extra moisture and nitrogen. The clippings don't cause thatch.

There are some instances, however, when it's really handy to have a bag attachment for your mower. For example, before you overseed a lawn, mow closely and catch the clippings so you don't have to rake them up to expose the bare soil. Moreover, if annual weeds, such as crabgrass, have formed seeds, a bag attachment will catch the seedheads along with the clippings and prevent self-seeding; throw the contents into the trash.

based on craftsmanship, design, and materials. Wherever possible, try them out to be sure they are comfortable to use and appropriate for your situation. Durability is an important factor, too, as are ease of maintenance, convenience, and safety features. Look for mowers that instantly shut off the mower blade when you release the handle baffle, and spreaders that will hang on a wall. The ultimate test of a tool's performance is its owner. Use all tools correctly —for your safety and for the health of your yard.

choosing the right mower

mower type	advantages	disadvantages
Push (reel) mower	■ Quiet, lightweight, maneuverable. ■ Easy to store. ■ Has superior cutting blades.	■ Hard to sharpen. ■ Operator must be in good physical condition. ■ Requires overlapping rows to ensure uniform cut.
Gasoline-powered, mulching rotary mower	■ Cuts clippings small, requiring no raking or bagging. ■ Easy to adjust cutting height. Mulches fallen leaves into lawn as topdressing. ■ Most offer self-propel, bag-attachment, and side- or back-discharge options. ■ Variety of horsepower ratings available.	■ Noisy and pollutes atmosphere. Needs frequent maintenance. Sometimes hard to start. ■ Needs periodic refueling, oil change, new spark plug.
Corded, electric-powered rotary mower	■ Non-polluting. ■ Cuts clippings small, requiring no raking or bagging. ■ Easy to adjust cutting height. ■ Mulches fallen leaves into lawn as topdressing. ■ Requires little maintenance. ■ Side/back discharge.	■ Noisy. ■ Cord can become a danger, as well as a nuisance, especially when mowing location is significant distance from electrical outlet.
Battery-rechargable electric rotary mower	■ No cord to worry about. ■ Fairly quiet. ■ No engine maintenance. ■ Cuts clippings small, requiring no raking or bagging. ■ Easy to adjust cutting height. ■ Mulches leaves into lawn as topdressing.	■ Must be plugged in between uses to recharge battery. ■ Bulky to maneuver. ■ Not available everywhere.
Riding mower	■ Covers large areas quickly. ■ Useful for operators with physical limitations. Automatic transmission, mulching blade, and cart options available.	■ Most expensive of all alternatives. ■ Requires larger storage area than others. ■ Repair and maintenance more extensive.

pruning tools

You need to prune trees and shrubs to keep them healthy. In fact, you may already routinely clip rubbing branches, shear hedges, remove an occasional injured or inconvenient tree limb, renovate old shrubs, and perform general grooming throughout your landscape. And if you live on a spacious, heavily wooded property, you occasionally may need to cut down a small tree, or cut up wood from one that has fallen. For each of these tasks there is a tool. Sometimes a simple hand tool does the job. In other instances, a powered version is your best choice. The trick is to know which one will help you do the job most efficiently. For example, don't use a hand pruner to cut thick

chainsaw safety

Because chainsaws are extremely dangerous, manufacturers go to great lengths to develop and equip them with many safety features. Never remove or disable chainbreaks, anti-kickback chain links, tip guards, or throttle interlocks, even though they seem to reduce efficiency.

hand pruner (bypass type)

Also known as secateurs, this pruner works one-handed. Its two steel blades bypass each other—the top, sharpened blade slices through twigs and stems up to ¾ inch thick. Some models have soft-grip or swivel handles.

hand pruner (anvil type)

Its sharpened top blade cuts by pressing twigs and stems against the thicker lower blade in a crushing, rather than slicing, action. Although this type isn't as versatile and maneuverable as a bypass pruner, it's more stable. And it requires less wrist and hand strength to operate.

hedge shears

This long-handled tool with 8- to 10-inch-long carbon steel blades cuts twigs and branches up to ½ inch thick. Use it to clip hedges and cut back ornamental grasses.

long-handled pruning saw

This 14- to 16-foot-long tool is ideal for pruning low-hanging tree branches up to 1½ inches thick. It typically has telescoping or extension handles made of wood or fiberglass. The very sharp steel saw at the tip easily slips between foliage-covered branches.

ratchet pruner

This type of pruner, although touted to cut almost anything, is best used on twigs and stems less than ½ inch thick. It was designed for people who lack the hand strength to operate other types of pruners. The racheting action allows you to keep squeezing the handles until the blades cut through the stem.

loppers

Essentially long-handled pruners, loppers require two hands to use. Available with bypass or anvil blades, they cut small branches and stems as thick as your thumb. They also extend your reach and give you improved cutting leverage.

branches or a saw to cut twigs. Pruning tools are sophisticated engineering marvels. The best ones—made of carbon steel, aluminum, and contemporary plastics—make pruning easy, as long as you care for them properly. Wipe off pruners, loppers, and saw blades after each use and sharpen them regularly.

Keep power tools clean and oiled. Store all tools indoors away from dampness. Look for extra features that improve the tools' performance. The best pruners and loppers have bumpers where their handles meet. Others have swivel handles, cushioned grips, and ratchet action to enhance your comfort.

compact pruning saw

The extremely sharp teeth on this compact, wooden-handled saw make quick work of medium-sized stems and branches. Those models that allow the blade to fold into the handle are equipped with a latch to prevent it from folding while you're using it.

bow pruning saw

The light weight of this saw makes it useful for cutting fallen branches. Its thin, toothed blade is attached at each end to a curved metal handle with a grip at one end. It quickly cuts any log that's no thicker than the length of the replaceable blade.

straight pruning saw

Once the workhorse for cutting major limbs, this straight-edged saw has been eclipsed by the chainsaw. But it still comes in handy when you don't want to get out the chainsaw to prune one or two large limbs. Some models offer a choice of coarse teeth on one edge, fine teeth on the other.

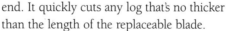

powered hedge clippers

Various models have 18- to 24-inch-long blades—the longer ones typically on heavy-duty models—with moveable cutting teeth. Some feature double blades that move in opposite directions to cut twiggy hedges more efficiently. The motor gets its power from an electrical cord or a portable battery pack.

chainsaw

Chainsaws cut with teeth linked together on a chain that's propelled around a grooved guide bar. They are powered by either a gasoline engine or electric motor at speeds up to 45 miles an hour.

watering tools

Shopping for a watering device can be quite a challenge. In fact, you can choose from literally dozens of models of sprinklers for just about any situation. Most are relatively inexpensive, so it makes sense to have several. Look for evidence of durable construction, because sprinklers have to endure a lot of abuse. They not only spend most of the summer in the hot sun, but they also suffer from hazards, such as run-ins with the family car, lawn mower, and children's play vehicles. Whatever the style of sprinkler, modern design offers several watering options. Many models feature mechanisms for adjusting the pattern, volume, angle, and direction of the water flow. Some are equipped

drip irrigation

Drip irrigation is the most efficient method of watering plants in the garden. By delivering water slowly and directly into the soil, it eliminates waste from evaporation or runoff. Plant leaves remain dry, therefore discouraging fungal disease. **Emitter systems** *feature intermittent nozzles along the pipe that deliver the water. They are good for rows of shrubs.* **Soaker (porous) hose systems** *leak water droplets along their entire length. They work well for closely planted flower, groundcover, or vegetable beds.*

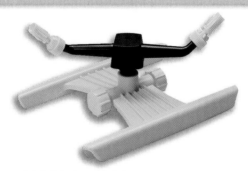

whirlybird sprinkler

As its nickname suggests, this rotating sprinkler throws water in a distinctive arcing pattern as its arm rotates from the force of the water coming out of the hose. Because the stream of water is interrupted by the action of the arm, it covers the areas both in the vicinity of the sprinkler and at some distance away from it. The spray is in larger droplets and falls fairly low to the ground.

fixed-spray sprinkler

Water from a fixed-spray sprinkler extends high into the air so it creates an umbrella pattern on small areas of groundcover or lawn. The fine, rain-like spray falls on foliage as well as soil, and some of the water is inevitably lost to evaporation in its travels. Choose a model with a stable base so it won't tip over.

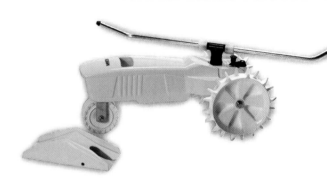

tractor sprinkler

As if it has a life of its own, this sprinkler travels as it delivers water. The force of the water propels the rotating sprinkler head on wheels guided by the hose. You can adjust the speed to vary the amount of water that reaches the area it traverses. Its watering pattern is not as wide as that of impulse sprinklers, but it's quite effective on broad, open lawns.

impulse sprinkler

Mounted on either a flat base, a tall tripod, or a spike you insert into the soil, these sprinklers throw rhythmic pulses of water over a wide area, relatively low to the ground. They can cover an area around their entire circumference or in just one sector. Water may reach as far as 100 feet away. They are ideal for lawns and under trees and shrubs. Their low arc minimizes evaporation.

with practical manual timers that shut them off automatically. Because most areas of the country have concerns about their fresh-water supplies, these timers help conserve water. An essential part of any watering system is the hose that supplies the water. Choose the best quality that you can afford. Look for a rubber or vinyl product that is constructed of several layers of mesh. The more substantial hoses are kink-free and hold up well against UV rays. Make sure yours has sturdy metal fittings to prevent leaks that waste water and reduce the effectiveness of the sprinkler.

pop-up sprinkler

This device is typically part of a professionally installed automated sprinkler system and is most common in warm areas of the country, where lawns require frequent moisture or on very large properties. The sprinkler head is permanently installed, flush with the ground. When the water is on, it pops up and sprays water in a fixed pattern. It can be programmed to deliver different amounts of water in different patterns.

oscillating sprinkler

Use this type to cover wide lawn areas or beds of tall plants best watered from above. It emits regular arching sprays of water from holes in its oscillating bar. You can adjust it to water on just one side in varying degrees or to swing in a full arc, from one side to another. On some models, you also can adjust the width of the spray patterns.

best times to water

Lawns – Water turfgrass deeply but infrequently. Wait until the grass indicates it needs it—turning dull and grayish. A footprint will remain hours after a person steps on it. The water-needed signal may happen just a few days after a watering where the soil is compacted or lacking moisture-holding organic matter. Water early in the day, so that the grass blades have time to dry off before nightfall. This discourages fungal disease.

Trees and shrubs – Water newly planted trees and shrubs every couple of days when rainfall is scarce and the weather is hot. Even long-established plants need water during droughts. Allow a hose to drip slowly at various spots under the foliage canopy to achieve deep watering over the broadly spreading root system. Be sure the mulch layer is not too thick; two or three inches will admit the water and then retard its evaporation from the soil. Water must penetrate at least 10 to 12 inches into the soil—the depth of most tree and shrub roots.

Flowers and vegetables – Annual plants, such as petunia, impatiens, nasturtium, basil, beans, and peas, are relatively shallow-rooted. Even when they're properly mulched, you'll need to water them every couple of days in dry, hot weather. Those in containers may need daily watering. Perennial plants, such as chrysanthemum, aster, pachysandra, astilbe, asparagus, and rhubarb, have deeper roots. In decent soil with proper mulch, they need water every five to eight days, depending on the heat. Water early in the day, so they have time to dry off by nightfall.

weeding tools

It seems that weeds are always with us. Their seeds lurk in the soil for decades, remaining viable, and lying in wait for a chance see some sun so they can germinate. Because some weeds typically produce up to 250,000 seeds from a single plant, it's no wonder that they are everywhere. Every time we disturb the soil—even when weeding—more seeds surface. That's why weeds are so common along roadsides and other edges where the soil is disturbed. Fortunately, you can discourage weeds by keeping the soil covered with dense groundcover plantings or mulch. Because the best defense is a good offense, go after weeds the minute they appear. Young ones are easier to

weather

Rainy weather is ideal for weeding. It's much easier to pull weeds from softened, moist soil than dry, hard soil. After the rain, wait until the moisture has a chance to soak deeply into the soil, then start pulling with a tool or by hand. In dry periods, water, then weed.

dandelion weeder

Also called a fishtail weeder, this traditional tool is designed to penetrate deeply into the soil to capture and pry out taproots of plants, such as dandelion and thistle. It is also useful for prying weeds from narrow spaces. You can buy it in either a short- or long-handled configuration. On the best models, the wooden handle is ergonomically shaped at a slight angle to give you an especially good grip. The notched blade at the tip is typically made of steel and has a sharp edge.

pronged-foot weeder

This heavy-duty tool is easy on the back. Sturdily fabricated from steel, it features a set of five round, pointed prongs mounted on a spring-loaded steel plate. This assembly is, in turn, attached to a larger steel foot plate with a tread on the back. Insert the prongs vertically into the soil by pushing on the waist-high wooden handle. Then step on the foot plate to lever the prongs upward, popping the weeds out of the soil.

crack weeder

This tool is part knife, part weeder. It's available in either long- or short-handled models and is strong and solid. The business end consists of an acutely angled steel tip that's thick and flat at its base, then tapers to a point as it curves upward. This weeder is ideal for levering shallow weeds from soil or scraping them from cracks in narrow spots between stones and in walks.

weed whip

This traditional tool was the original weed whacker. It has a wooden hand grip on a strong metal shank that's angled so its metal cutting piece is flat to the ground. The cutting piece is serrated on both edges so it cuts whether you're moving it forward or backward. Swing the whip—a mini scythe—much the way you would a golf club to cut tall rangy weeds down to size.

eliminate than older ones that have well-established root systems. Make every effort to deal with weeds before they set seed. Most are easiest to pull when they are flowering and just beginning to set seed.

❧ Tools give you the satisfaction of removing weeds immediately. Unlike herbicide sprays, which take hours or days to work, mechanical devices offer instant results. The trick is to get the root. In the case of perennial weeds, any piece of root left in the soil is likely to create a new weed. Use herbicides only on extensive patches of weeds or for harmful ones, such as poison ivy.

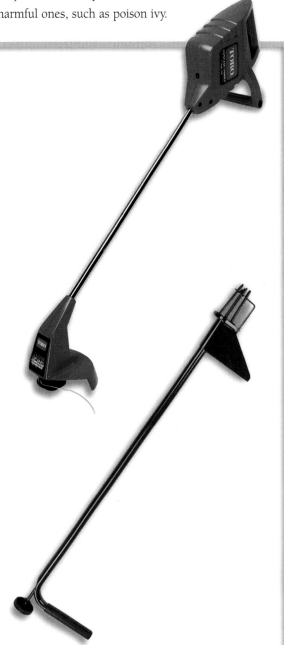

power weed trimmer

Power weed trimmers typically have an electric motor—either corded or battery-operated—but may be gas-powered, as well. They power a whirling piece of nylon string that resembles fishing line. As it continuously feeds off its spool at high speed, the line knocks off the tops of grassy weeds. It's especially useful along walls and drives. When you tilt it, this type of trimmer will edge around stepping stones and along walks. Replacement spools of nylon line are readily available. Take care not to use it too close to trees or shrubs—it's easy to cut the bark or stems, injuring or killing the plants.

dandelion weeder

This high-tech version of the traditional fishtail weeder is easier on the back. It has a waist-high handle of wood or steel, tipped by a ring of steel prongs. Center it over the weed and apply pressure to the foot plate attached to the base of the handle. This action inserts the prongs into the soil. Then use the knob or lever mechanism at the top of the wooden handle to trip the levered action, closing the prongs and trapping the crown of the plant. Finally, tug on the handle to pop the weed out, root and all.

fertilizers

Fertilizer is often called plant food but is actually soil food. It adds fresh supplies of nitrogen, phosphorus, and potassium to soil where these naturally occurring nutrients have been depleted. In areas where plants have been growing for a long time or are planted repeatedly, such as lawns, flower beds, and vegetable plots, the plants use up the primary nutrients over time. Plants that are expected to produce flowers or fruits continuously over an entire season use up soil nutrients faster than even the most fertile soil can provide. Fertilizer fills the deficiencies; it's not a substitute for healthy soil. Thin, compacted soil that has virtually no organic matter needs a lot of help

plant nutrition

Plants require three major nutrients: nitrogen (N), phosphorus (P), and potassium (K).

Nitrogen *fuels leaf and stem growth and is the the nutrient that's most quickly depleted (especially in lawns).*

Phosphorus *stimulates root growth and seed formation and is prominent in fertilizers used in fall.*

Potassium *promotes flowering, fruiting, and disease resistance.*

1 When preparing a new garden bed, cultivate the soil first. Sprinkle granular, slow-acting fertilizer on the soil, following label instructions, then rake it in.

from fertilizer if it's to do anything more than hold plants up. Fortunately, you can reduce the amount of fertilizer you'll need in future years by amending the soil by adding organic matter every year. The resulting rich, fertile soil needs less help from fertilizer. Look for fertilizers that are slow-acting and granular. For general use, choose those labeled "balanced" or "all-purpose." You can buy specialty products for certain groups of plants, such as lawns, roses, acid-loving trees and shrubs, bulbs, and vegetables. Their formulations are adjusted to the needs of these plant groups.

fertilize with caution

Keep this advice in mind whenever you are using fertilizers.

- Avoid overuse of fertilizers.
- Water plants and lawns well before using water-soluble products.
- Delay fertilizing newly planted trees and shrubs for a year.
- Do not fertilize plants stressed by drought, disease, or pests.
- Do not fertilize and lime the lawn simultaneously.

151

2 The action of a rototiller incorporates granular fertilizer into the soil down 4 to 6 inches. Follow label instructions for the amount of fertilizer to use.

3 Spread fertilizer on beds in early spring to supply plants with uniform and consistent nutrition for up to 16 weeks—a good main meal.

4 Follow the application of granular, slow-acting fertilizer with periodic snacks of water-soluble fertilizer. Spray it directly on foliage (foliar feeding) with a hose-end sprayer or spray bottle, to deliver a quick boost to plants about to flower or fruit. Follow label directions for dilution ratios to avoid harmful overfeeding.

fertilizers (cont'd.)

Container-grown plants require special fertilizers, because planting mixes intended for container use are typically soil-less—lighter, disease-free, and devoid of nutrients. Unless the manufacturer chose to add slow-acting fertilizer—an action that, fortunately, is becoming more common—you must provide all the nutrition to your container plants, whether they are indoor or outdoor, ornamental or food. Fertilizers are sometimes categorized as organic or synthetic. Both provide the same nutrition, but they vary in their sources of nutrients and the way the nutrients are released into the soil. The nutrients in synthetic fertilizers are

Coverage

Although lawn fertilizer is packaged by weight, that is not an indication of how much you need. Look for a phrase on the label indicating how many square feet the bag's contents cover.

Water-soluble fertilizer

Water-soluble fertilizer is delivered with moisture. Its nitrogen acts very quickly but only for a short time. You need to apply it repeatedly to provide uniform, continuous nutrition.

NPK Ratio

These numbers indicate the relative proportion of nitrogen, phosphorus, and potassium—the major nutrients in the product. Lawn fertilizer is always heavy in nitrogen.

Type of fertilizer

Each fertilizer label prominently indicates the type of fertilizer. It may use the terms, "lawn," "houseplant," "nursery" (for trees and shrubs), or similar language.

Guaranteed analysis

The "guaranteed analysis" box indicates the kinds and percentages of nutrients in the formulation. A large proportion of WIN, or water-insoluble nitrogen, means it's slow-acting.

1198-1012

NET WT. 5 LBS.

Miracle-Gro LAWN FOOD

36-6-6

GUARANTEED ANALYSIS

Total Nitrogen (N) 36%
  1.2% Ammoniacal Nitrogen
  1.9% Nitrate Nitrogen
  32.9% Urea Nitrogen
Available Phosphate (P_2O_5) 6%
Soluble Potash (K_2O) 6%
Iron (Fe) 0.325%
  0.325% Chelated Iron

Nitrogen derived from Ammonium Phosphate; Potassium Nitrate and Urea; Phosphate derived from Ammonium Phosphate; Potash derived from Potassium Nitrate; Iron derived from Iron EDTA.

SCOTTS MIRACLE-GRO PRODUCTS, INC.
P.O. BOX 888, PORT WASHINGTON, NY 11050

EASY SPRINKLER-WAY TO A SPRINGTIME GREEN LAWN ALL SUMMER LONG

Try the Miracle-Gro® No-Clog™ 4 in 1 Lawn and Garden Feeder attached to your sprinkler!

SAVE TIME! SAVE WORK! Apply Miracle-Gro Water Soluble Lawn Food through your sprinkler with the Miracle-Gro No-Clog™ 4 in 1 Lawn and Garden Feeder. Water and feed at the same time!

YOU'LL SEE RESULTS FAST- often within two or three days after application. By following a regular schedule of feeding and watering, you can have a green "showplace" lawn throughout the summer.

Set up diagram for the "Sprinkler - Feeder Method"

manufactured from chemicals. In slow-acting products, they are coated to prevent them from immediately dissolving in water. They break down in moist soil gradually, so they are available over time to the plants. The nutrients in organic products are derived from natural plant and animal sources, such as manures, wood, paper, fish and bone meal, and seaweed. The activity of microbes in the soil releases the nutrients and makes them available to the plants.

Reading the numbers
In balanced, all-purpose fertilizers, the numbers that indicate the ratio of the basic nutrients—nitrogen, phosphorus, and potassium (NPK)—are typically much closer together numerically.

153

All-purpose fertilizer
All-purpose fertilizers are appropriate for many kinds of plants. They have a wide variety of nutrients, including the major ones, plus micro nutrients and trace minerals.

How much to use
Different plants need different amounts of nutrients. Carefully follow label instructions for diluting fast-acting, water-soluble products to avoid harming the plant and the soil.

Frequency of feeding
Plant roots and leaves quickly take up the nitrogen in water-soluble fertilizers. It rapidly greens up their foliage. However, because it's also used up quickly, it requires repeat doses.

Don't overfeed
Over-fertilizing a plant stresses it. Too much nitrogen encourages overproduction of tender foliage that tempts pest insects. The result: stalled fruit or flower production.

NET WT. 5 LBS. STERN'S Miracle-Gro 15-30-15

GUARANTEED ANALYSIS

Total Nitrogen (N) 15%
  6.8% Ammoniacal Nitrogen
  8.2% Urea Nitrogen
Available Phosphoric Acid (P$_2$O$_5$) 30%
Soluble Potash (K$_2$O) 15%
Boron (B) 0.02%
Copper (Cu) 0.07%
Iron (Fe) 0.15%
  0.15% Chelated Iron
Manganese (Mn) 0.05%
  0.05% Chelated Manganese
Molybdenum (Mo) 0.0005%
Zinc (Zn) 0.06%

Nitrogen from Ammonium Phosphates and Urea; Phosphoric Acid from Ammonium Phosphates; Potash from Muriate of Potash; Boron from Boric Acid; Copper from Copper Sulfate; Chelated Iron from Iron EDTA; Manganese from Manganese EDTA; Molybdenum from Sodium Molybdate; Zinc from Zinc Sulfate. Chlorine (Max. Avail.) 12.5%

STERN'S MIRACLE-GRO PRODUCTS, INC.
Port Washington, N.Y. 11050 U.S.A.
FLLN 720-1013

SUGGESTED FEEDING INSTRUCTIONS

TYPE OF PLANT	AMOUNT OF MIRACLE-GRO SOLUTION	HOW OFTEN
ROSES— Large bushes— (Spreading over 2 ft.)	ONE GALLON per bush	Every 2 weeks
ROSES— Medium & small plants (Less than 2 ft. wide)	½ to ONE GALLON per bush	Every 2 weeks
ALL FLOWERS	ONE GALLON per 10 square feet	Every 7-14 days
ALL VEGETABLES	ONE GALLON per 10 square feet	Every 7-14 days
TOMATOES	ONE GALLON per plant	Every 7-14 days
TREES Fruit & Ornamental	ONE GALLON per 10 square feet Soak soil	3 times a year
BERRIES and other small fruits	ONE GALLON per 10 square feet	Every 2-4 weeks
EVERGREENS Broadleaf and needle-leaved types	ONE GALLON per 10 square feet	Every 2 weeks
DECIDUOUS SHRUBS (Drops leaves in winter)	ONE GALLON per 10 square feet	Every 2 weeks
LAWNS	ONE GALLON per 25 square feet	Every 4 weeks

DON'T WASTE MIRACLE-GRO. Small, newly-planted plants need just enough plant food to wet their root areas.

how to read a plant tag

Plant tags are full of information to help you make the best choice at your garden center or nursery. Take the time to examine them and learn about the specific requirements of the plants they accompany. By means of symbols and pictures, growers pack as many facts and details as possible onto the small plastic tag—to help you successfully grow and nurture your plants.

Typically, the front of a tag lists the plant's common and scientific names and summarizes key information about it. An accompanying close-up color photo usually shows the plant's flowers and foliage as they appear at maturity. Once in a while, the photo shows the entire plant in a garden setting to

Appearance at maturity

The color photo shows you how the plant will look when it's full-grown. This is a big help, because the best time to buy plants is when they are young—often before flowers are visible.

Lighting preferences

Look for a symbol to indicate the type of light the plant requires. This one means full sun. Other symbols are used to indicate partial shade and shade.

Special details

Check the description of the plant's characteristics, foliage, and the type of soil and climate it prefers. Special qualities, such as drought tolerance, may be mentioned.

Common names

Labels typically highlight a plant's common name. Because they vary from region to region, the scientific name, too—in Latin—to be sure of its exact identity.

Size at maturity

Note the plant's expected height and width (or spread) at maturity. These details will help you avoid the need to prune it constantly or eventually move the plant because it's too large for its space.

Expertise required

Some plants are more difficult to grow than others. Check the label for an icon that indicates that the plant is appropriate to your gardening skill and interest level.

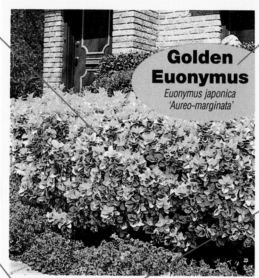

Better Homes and Gardens

Golden Euonymus

Euonymus japonica 'Aureo-marginata'

Full sun | **10' Tall 5' Wide** | **Easy to grow** | **Low maintenance**

- Attractive and colorful evergreen shrub
- Showy leaves with golden margins
- Tolerant of high heat and unfavorable soil conditions
- Nice foundation or mass planting

$00.00

0 08776 51512 4

5 GAL. GLEAF

help you judge its relative size and potential use in your yard. Symbols on the tag give size information, as well as sun, soil, and water requirements. And you might find desirable features, listed as bulleted phrases. The reverse side of the tag is usually devoted to more specific details on how to transplant and care for the plant—information that's especially critical to the survival of perennials, trees, and shrubs. The tags that accompany plants you buy will be a valuable reference over many seasons as the plants grow and bloom. Save, date and store the tags somewhere handy.

Cold-hardiness range
Perennial plants, trees, and shrubs vary in their ability to withstand winter weather. Check the label for their geographical cold-hardiness range, indicated by zone numbers.

Planting instructions
Because plants often have specific planting needs, read and follow the step-by-step planting instructions. For instance, various bulbs need to be planted at specific soil depths.

Proper spacing
Spacing information is very helpful when you make your buying decisions—especially for plants you intend as groundcovers or hedges.

Other helpful products
Some tags suggest products that reduce plant stress during transplanting and afterward. A few examples are water-saving crystals, kelp or seaweed tonics, and mycorrhiza products.

Care advice
Plant tags often offer guidance on care of the plant after you've planted it Proper watering, fertilizing, and pruning are critical to its vigor and beauty.

COLD HARDINESS

USDA
Zones 6-9

This plant is generally hardy in the colored areas shown
0649

PLANTING GUIDE

Plant in full sun in moist, well-drained, fertile soil. A 2-4" layer of mulch is beneficial.

Space plants 4-5' apart

1. **Dig** hole slightly larger than plant's root mass or pot size.
2. **Backfill** hole with a finely crumbled mound of freshly dug soil. To remove plant, tap pot edge on a hard surface, then ease plant out of pot. If root mass is tightly tangled, loosen exposed surface with fingers or a sharp knife.
3. **Place** root mass on top of backfilled soil so that it is high enough to place plant's main stem at its original soil depth. Backfill with remaining soil. Tamp soil gently.
4. **Water** deeply immediately. Apply a root-stimulator solution according to package directions.
5. **Mulch** around plant leaving breathing space between mulch and plant base.

We recommend:
MIRACLE-GRO
QUICK START

- **Helps prevent transplant shock.**
- **Stimulates new root growth.**

"LIFE INSURANCE" FOR PLANTS

BUY WITH CONFIDENCE
All trees and Shrubs Guaranteed by Wal-Mart®

CARE AND MAINTENANCE

Water in the morning with a hose or drip system that saturates the area around the drip line. Water when the soil is dry 3-4" deep.

Prune before new growth begins in spring or in late fall.

Apply fertilizer in early spring just before new growth begins.

composting

Making compost is a most satisfying way to recycle your yard debris and improve your soil. A collection of fallen leaves, weeds, prunings, other yard waste, and non-meat kitchen scraps will decompose in a corner of your yard just the way they do in nature. In the presence of air and moisture, the teeming populations of microscopic fungi, bacteria, and other organisms that live on plant surfaces break down these collected materials. As they feed and reproduce in an elaborate food chain, they gradually transform organic waste into dark, crumbly compost. If you are in no hurry to harvest compost, just continually pile up yard debris as it accumulates and let it set in a heap. After a year or

making leaf mold

If the yard debris on your property consists mostly of leaves, you can make leaf mold, which is similar to compost. Collect the leaves in a pile, moisten them, and wait for them to decompose partially. If you shred them or go over them with a mulching mover first, they will break down more quickly.

Rotate the drum to stir composting materials in these tumbler-style composters. Turn the drum opening downward to empty the finished compost into a garden cart positioned under the drum.

A pile of green and brown organic waste decomposes gradually if left undisturbed. Add fresh waste to the top; harvest compost from the bottom.

A triple bin is most convenient for a more active composting system. Turn the pile into the next bin when it reaches peak internal heat.

so, you'll be able to dig under the pile and harvest a few bushels of compost. This passive method takes very little effort. ❧On the other hand, if your goal is to make as much compost as possible as fast as you can, cut or chop the raw materials first, turn the pile periodically, and add composting worms. This active method requires a lot more time and effort, but it yields compost in a matter of weeks. ❧Use compost to improve the texture and moisture-holding capacity of the soil on your property. It loosens heavy clay and bulks up sandy soil. And it revitalizes microlife in the soil.

❧Finished compost resembles dark, rich soil. It's lightweight and has a pleasant, woodsy smell. Mix it into the soil to improve its drainage.

dos and don'ts of composting

- Do clip, shred, or chop materials into smaller, roughly uniform-sized pieces for faster decomposition.
- Do put coarser materials, such as sticks, corncobs, pinecones, and similar items, in a pile of their own for more even decomposition.
- Do use peanut hulls, straw, shredded paper, and sawdust (from non-treated wood).
- Do make sure that brown (dry) materials are in far greater proportion than green (moist) materials to prevent your pile from smelling.
- Do take advantage of local materials beyond the yard, such as farm-animal bedding, wood chips, fruit and vegetable trimmings, nut hulls, grape skins, and seaweed.
- Don't put meat or meat products, salad dressings, butter, or other fats in the pile.
- Don't include diseased plants or weeds with seeds.
- Don't include human feces or used kitty litter.

mulching

The best way to protect the bare soil on your property is to mulch it. A layer of organic material several inches thick buffers the soil against compaction from the harsh effects of heavy rain and baking sun and helps the soil retain oxygen so it can support vigorous plant roots. It improves any soil by blending valuable organic material, or humus, into its top layer as the mulch gradually decomposes. In nature, soil is always protected by a covering of organic material. Layers of leaf litter in the woods and blankets of waving grasses on the plains prevent erosion and absorb rainfall, just as your lawn and groundcover beds do. A layer of organic mulch provides similar protection to soil

weather

During the winter, fluctuating temperatures alternately freeze and thaw the soil. This often disturbs plant roots and may heave bulbs or plants out of the soil. A winter mulch does not prevent soil from freezing, but it provides insulation to maintain more even low temperatures.

A good way to recycle fallen leaves is to use them to mulch bare soil all around the yard. Shred or chop them so they don't mat and block water from the soil.

Buckwheat or hulls from pecans, cocoa beans, and other nuts make a uniform, colorful mulch for small garden areas. They are particularly attractive under low, fine-textured plants.

Gravel is an appropriate mulch for arid landscapes and beds with plants that need good drainage, such as rock gardens.

Pine needles provide a handsome, brown covering for the soil. Use them around acid-loving plants such as conifers, rhododendrons, and hollies.

that *isn't* covered by plants. In your landscape, it forms an attractive cover that discourages weeds and masks imperfections. More importantly, it helps conserve water by absorbing rainfall and preventing runoff. Soil covered by a layer of organic mulch stays damp much longer between rains or waterings because the mulch blocks evaporation. ❧Mulch protects nearby plants, too. A good layer of organic mulch between newly planted groundcover plants discourages weeds during the time the plants need to grow larger, knit together, and cover the soil on their own. ❧Trees and shrubs

❧River rocks used as mulch suggest rocky shorelines or dry riverbeds in landscape settings. On sunny sites, they retain warmth, creating a microclimate around the plants. They also allow air access to the soil. On the minus side, they don't do a very good job of discouraging weeds.

mulching (cont'd.)

thrive on mulch, too. Circles of organic material under them not only condition the soil and improve its fertility, but they also create a barrier to prevent injury to their trunks and stems from lawn mowers and string trimmers. A layer of organic mulch on the bare soil in your yard also contributes to the general health and vigor of the entire landscape because it shelters many kinds of beneficial organisms. For example, ground spiders and ants nest in rich organic material along the edges of lawns. From there, they prey on pest insect larvae and eggs in the soil under the lawn and garden beds. Avoid spreading mulch too thickly. Anything over

mulching trees and shrubs

A layer of organic mulch over the root zone of newly planted trees and shrubs helps them get off to a good start. Cover the entire area where the soil was disturbed and is bare. This will prevent weeds from sprouting and competing with newly developing plant roots for soil moisture and nutrients. It also helps keep soil moist during the critical early growth period.

Shredded paper makes a suitable mulch for protecting soil and discouraging weeds. If it becomes unsightly when rains wet it down, cover it with a thin layer of leaves or bark nuggets.

Leaf mold (partially decomposed leaves) contributes valuable organic matter to the soil as it continues to decompose. Use it for plants in woodland settings and informal gardens.

Wood chips are long-lasting—andinexpensive, if you can persuade a landscaper to drop them off for free. Allow them to age for a few weeks, then spread them on paths and under trees and woody plants.

Cocoa bean shells offer a fine-textured, uniform covering, plus a wonderful smell—especially after a rain. Their rich brown color contrasts beautifully with turfgrasses and colorful groundcovers.

2 or 3 inches threatens to become a suffocating blanket that blocks air and moisture from the soil. This causes plant roots to gravitate toward the soil surface in search of these essentials. In cases where surface tree roots are a problem, mulch lightly to improve the appearance of the yard, but don't try to bury the roots. Organic mulch inevitably breaks down over time, and the mulch layer becomes thinner. Expect to add to it periodically, usually in the fall, to restore it to a 2- to 3-inch depth.

mulching a tree

1 When you mulch an established tree with grass growing beneath it, put a layer of cardboard over the lawn before spreading the mulch. This will keep the grass from penetrating the mulch.

2 Make the cardboard collar at least 2 or 3 feet wide. Moisten it so it softens and conforms to the contours of the ground and the root flare at the base of the trunk. Then cover it with wood chips.

3 Limit the mulch layer to 2 or 3 inches, so that the tree roots still can get sufficient air and moisture. Otherwise, they will migrate toward the soil surface. Be very careful not to pile mulch against the tree trunk. Unlike root bark, trunk bark can't handle constant moisture and will rot. If you feel so inclined, add a border of bricks, rocks, or other attractive material around the collar.

plant list

It's a good idea to keep track of the plants in your garden

It helps you remember what's planted where. Photocopy this page, if you wish, to start a garden journal. Here you may keep records of each plant you buy, the date, and where you plant it. The comments column is for any other information you want to remember, such as where you bought it, the date it bloomed, how long it stayed in bloom, the color of the flower, and pest or disease problems. You'll find that this type of record-keeping is helpful as your garden matures, allowing you to remember all its pertinent facts and history. Some people also record when (if) a plant dies, and why.

plant name	date planted	location

comments

plant resources

Mail-Order Nurseries

key
(B) bulbs
(P) plants
(S) seeds

Antique Rose Emporium (P) free
9300 Lueckemeyer Rd.
Brenham, TX 77833–6453
800-441-0002
www.antiqueroseemporium.com

Arena Rose Co. (P) $5.00
P.O. Box 3096
Paso Robles, CA 93447
805-227-4094

Brent and Becky's Bulbs (B) free
7463 Heath Trail
Gloucester, VA 23061
804-693-3966
www.BrentandBecky'sbulb.com

Forestfarm (P) $4.00
990 Tetherow Rd.
Williams, OR 97544-9599
541-846-7269
www.forestfarm.com

Greer Gardens (P) $3.00
1280 Goodpasture Island Road
Eugene, OR 97401
541-686-8266
www.greergardens.com

Heronswood Nursery Ltd. (P) $5.00
7530 NE 288th St.
Kingston, WA 98346
360-297-4172
www.Heronswood.com

Jackson & Perkins Co. (P) free
53 Rose Lane
Medford, OR 97501
800-292-4769
www.jacksonandperkins.com

Kurt Bluemel, Inc. (P) $3.00
2740 Greene Ln.
Baldwin, MD 21013–9523
800-248-7584
www.Bluemel.com

Louisiana Nursery (P) $5.00
5853 Highway 182
Opelousas, LA 70570
318-948-3696

Mountain Maples (P) $2.00
P.O. Box 1329
Laytonville, CA 95454
707-984-6522
www.mountainmaples.com

Musser Forests (P) free
P.O. Box S-91 M
Indiana, PA 15701
800-643-3819
www.musserforests.com

Niche Gardens (P) $3.00
1111 Dawson Rd.
Chapel Hill, NC 27516
919-967-0078
www.nichegdn.com

Plant Delights Nursery (P) $3.00
9241 Sauls Rd.
Raleigh, NC 27603
919-772-4794
www.plantdel.com

Roslyn Nursery (P) $2.00
211 Burns Lane
Dix Hills, NY 11746
516-643-9347
www.roslynnursery.com

Stark Bros. Nursery (P) Free
P.O. Box 10
Louisiana, MO 63353
573-754-5511
www.Starkbros.com

Van Bourgondien (P) free
P.O. Box 1000
Babylon, NY 11702
800-622-9997
www.vanbourgondien.com

White Flower Farm (P) free
P.O. Box 50
Litchfield, CT 06759–0050
800-503-9624
www.whiteflowerfarm.com

Woodlanders (P) $2.00
1128 Colleton Ave.
Aiken, SC 29801
803-648-7522

Yard and Garden Supplies

Duncraft Specialities for Birds
102 Fisherville Road
Concord, NH 03303-2086
800-593-5656
www.duncraft.com

Gardener's Supply Company
128 Intervale Road
Burlington, VT 05401
800-955-3370
www.gardenerssupply.com

Kinsman Co.
River Road
Point Pleasant, PA 18950
803-733-4146
www.kinsmangarden.com

Lagenbach Tools free
638Lindero Canyon Road, MSC 290
Oak Park, CA 91301-5464
800-362-1991
www.langenbach.com

Plants from the Internet

http://www.bhglive.com
http://www.garden.com
http://www.landscapeusa.com

index

index (cont'd.)